A Year in the
Country

ANGELIC FAVOR BOX TEMPLATES

Use photocopier to enlarge patterns 200%
(see p. 190 for instructions)

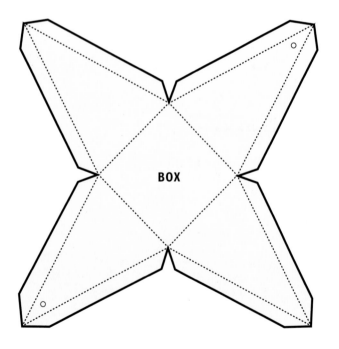

BOX

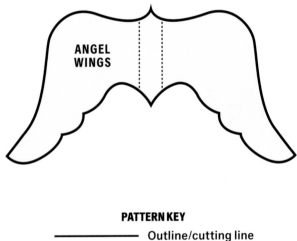

ANGEL WINGS

PATTERN KEY

——————— Outline/cutting line

---------------- Score line

Table of Contents

SPRING

SUMMER

AUTUMN

WINTER

Front Cover
Oak trees and mustard plants, Ron and Patty Thomas/Getty Images

Title Page
Pemaquid Point Lighthouse, Terry Donnelly

A Country Book

© 2023 RDA Enthusiast Brands, LLC.
1610 N. 2nd St., Suite 102
Milwaukee, WI 53212-3906

ISBN
978-1-62145-938-5

Component Number
116800110H

We are committed to both the quality of our products and the service we provide to our customers. We value your comments, so please feel free to contact us at *TMBBookTeam@TrustedMediaBrands.com*.

Text, photography and illustrations for *A Year in the Country* are based on articles previously published in *Country, Country Woman, Farm & Ranch Living*, and *Birds & Blooms* magazines.

HELLO!

The pace of rural living invites us all to slow down and breathe deep. There's time to really smell the flowers, contemplate the ripples in a pond, lend a hand to our neighbor, sit down to supper with family and friends.

The pages of this book invite you to do all that—and to savor so many of the other simple joys that rural life has to offer. You'll find stories and photos of farming, family, favorite barnyard pals, tractors and the peace that's found in a walk through the woods. You'll also discover time-tested family recipes and easy craft ideas—all gathered from the readers of *Country*, *Country Woman*, *Farm & Ranch Living* and *Birds & Blooms* magazines.

No matter your connection to our rural landscapes, whether you work the land, dream of doing so one day, or just prefer a quiet gravel road to a busy highway, this book is sure to take you there. So settle in, and breathe deep.

THE EDITORS

Wildflowers on a hillside along the Kebler Pass near Crested Butte, Colorado.

PHOTO BY ANDREW SOUNDARAJAN/ GETTY IMAGES

Spring

The Good Life

LLAMARAMA!

Three generations of farmers transform their
llamas' fleece into colorful yarns and accessories

JODY PETER FORT ATKINSON, WI

Welcome to Stone Crest Llamas, our family operation in southern Wisconsin. The two farms are owned by my husband, Gregg Peter, and me; our two children, ages 9 and 11; and my parents, Glenn and Joyce Laird. We are fortunate to live across the street from my mom and dad, and we often move the llamas between farms. Gregg and I also work full time off the farm, so life is busy! We raise llamas, miniature Nubian dairy goats, poultry and rabbits. We take pride in growing a lot of our food in gardens and on fruit trees—to go with all the fresh eggs and goat milk.

This all began in 1991 when I was 11. I did a science fair project about llamas, and my parents made the mistake of taking me to a farm that raised llamas to learn more about them. I fell in love that day and my mom did, too. Little did we know that this would be the start of an amazing partnership. As a kid I had horses, donkeys, goats, chickens and rabbits, so adding a few llamas to the farm seemed to fit into my folks' life just fine. Our small herd of three slowly grew to 30. My mom and I learned to process fleeces and turn them into various products, and we learned to spin, felt and weave.

In 2005, Gregg and I purchased our first farm. We added breeding stock with good conformation; fine fleece characteristics and calm, easy-to-handle personalities. We focused on marketing and expanding the fiber side of raising llamas. Today the entire family is involved.

We love raising our kids in the country. Both of them are in 4-H and show their animals at the local county fair. This teaches so much responsibility and a love for animals. My son raises call ducks and English Orpington chickens. He also owns a yearling mini Nubian goat named Luna. My daughter has Ameraucana chickens, Holland Lop rabbits and a mini Nubian named April. Both enjoy the fiber arts and often make items to sell at our annual open house. Gregg makes fences and builds stalls and pens, things that are especially helpful. He and his dad also make hay, which feeds the animals all winter. His parents have an organic crop farm.

Llamas are easy livestock to raise. They rarely get sick and eat amounts similar to our miniature dairy goats. They are wonderful mothers and birth easily, with each doe typically producing one offspring per year. They have soft padded feet that do not wreck pastures. And keeping the barn clean is easy because they go to the bathroom in set spots. The manure is high in nutrients, perfect for gardens and flower beds. Llamas do require annual shearing and vaccinations, routine deworming and nail trimmings as needed.

People always ask why we raise llamas. For us, the main reason is to harvest their fine, silk-like fiber, which is generally softer than sheep's wool. Yarn made from camelids (llamas and alpacas) is popular for knitting and crocheting because it is

Little did we know that this would be the start of an amazing partnership.

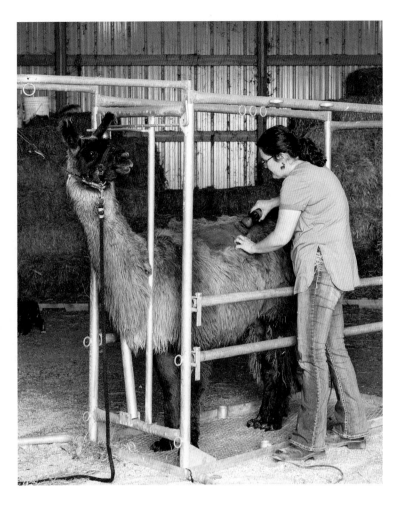

strong, soft and warm. This fire-resistant fiber also has a hollow core center that wicks away moisture. Because llama fiber doesn't contain lanolin, an oil found in sheep's wool, it's often the go-to product for people with wool allergies.

Fiber processing is a big part of our operation. We run a farm store in our basement where we sell wool products such as roving, yarn, socks, hats, mittens, rugs, blankets, dryer balls, insoles and felted artwork. Each fall we have an open house and multiple yarn crawls that bring in many visitors.

MAMA LLAMAS & THEIR BABIES
April 15 Last week one of our mini Nubians kidded a doe that soon began bouncing around the pasture with the herd. A mini Nubian mom produces around a gallon of milk per day for the first eight to 10 weeks, most of which goes to her kid. But after weaning, she is milked twice a day and we get to keep the milk.

Left: Gregg and Jody Peter with their children and Jody's parents, Glenn and Joyce. Above: Jody gives one of the show llamas a fresh barrel cut.

The Peter children live the farm life to its fullest. Both are involved in 4-H and raise ducks, chickens, rabbits and miniature Nubian goats.

April 16 The veterinarian came out today to disbud our new doe kid. Disbudding prevents young goats from growing horns and later getting stuck in our fencing or causing injury to another goat. We also had the vet check three male llamas that we plan to show, so we'll be able to provide the required health certificates.

April 17 Since the pasture has started to grow, the llamas and goats are grazing on grass and eating less hay. That means it's time to take the extra hay from around the round bale feeders and use it to mulch our vegetable gardens.

April 18 We planted shade trees in our pastures so the animals have more shade on hot summer days. We also burned off dried grasses from our 4-acre female pasture. This helps control invasive weeds. In a few weeks, green shoots will pop up that the llamas will love eating.

April 19 We are watching for crias (baby llamas) because three females are due any day. The stalls have been freshly bedded; we keep crias in them with their moms for the first 24 hours to make sure they're bonded and nursing well.

April 20 Our warmer spring weather left us today. With snow flurries, it feels like winter is back. Still no new babies—somewhat of a relief in this cold.

April 21 We woke up to another cold morning—only 27 degrees. When I did my regular morning check on the animals, I noticed two of our pregnant female llamas were humming, which meant they would likely be birthing soon. In almost 30 years of raising llamas, I had never experienced two crias being born on the same day. That changed today.

Reba delivered a 23-pound female in the field around noon. It was cold, so we brought the pair into the barn, dipped the baby's navel, towel-dried her and used a hair dryer to help finish the job and keep her warm. We then weighed her (as we do for each cria), so we can monitor her for weight gain. Then we put her in a coat and left her in the stall with Reba so they could bond. Reba seemed stressed and unwilling to stand to let her baby nurse, so we gave the cria some colostrum and hoped she'd be nursing by morning. Fiona delivered a 29-pound male around 7 p.m. We repeated the warming process and put him in a second stall with Fiona. A patient first-time mother, she doted on him.

SHEARING TIME & SHOW PREP

April 22 I was happy to find the female cria nursing this morning. Sometimes just leaving them alone is best for bonding. The male hadn't started nursing yet, though his dam was standing for him. He didn't seem too bright—at one point I found him sucking on the wall—so I gave him a bottle to keep him strong. Then I let everyone out in the sun to be with the herd. By afternoon the air was warmer, Fiona had come into her milk, her baby was nursing and all was good. At dusk we brought them back into the stalls. We'll do this for the first few cold nights.

April 23 We let the new crias out with the herd, and they started to play and explore. Reba, an excellent guard, chased a cat who wanted to meet the new arrivals. She was not thrilled, either, with the duck that wanted to make a nest in the barn.

April 24 We shear annually as a way to help keep our llamas cooler in the summer heat. The process started today with the show llamas, because the first big llama show of the season is coming fast. Each got a barrel cut around the midsection that left the neck and legs alone so the quality of the animal's fiber can be judged. We'll sort the shorn wool, wash it and make it into yarn—some for selling by the skein, some for making into socks.

April 25 Today we started shearing the breeding females. We often shear the entire body to keep them cooler and give us more fleece to process. We also trimmed the llamas' toenails, vaccinated them and treated them with a dewormer to prevent meningeal worms. The worms can cause severe neurological damage that requires aggressive treatment and sometimes leads to euthanasia. We treat the llamas monthly with the preventative, since our area has a high number of deer that can spread the worms to llamas.

April 26 Our last spring baby llama—a 29-pound female—was born today at about 2 p.m. Ebony, the mom, got up quickly and nursed her baby out in the pasture. Since it was a warm day, we left the baby llama out with the herd until dusk. Then we brought the mom and baby into a stall overnight to give the little one's legs time to strengthen.

April 27 I spent the day washing buckets and packing show halters, hay bags and other show supplies into the trailer. I also haltered the three males, did a short grooming session and helped them practice leading and standing. They did well.

April 28 Our mini Nubian buck went to a new home this morning. The buyer came out to learn more about caring for goats and how we manage the herd. This buck will produce beautiful kids for the new buyer. In the afternoon we bathed the two weanling males—I think I got just as wet as they did!

COMPETING OUT OF STATE

April 29 We finished packing the trailer to go to Indiana for a national show called March Llama Madness. Readying the animals for show takes quite a bit of time and dedication. I also bathed our breeding-age male llama. He did great!

April 30 My parents will feed and care for the animals—and our human children—while Gregg and I travel to Indiana with three llamas for the weekend. This show, one of the biggest in the country, will have about 400 llamas and breeders from 25 states. We look forward to seeing friends from all over

Left: Processed and dyed llama wool. Right: Jody's mom hand-makes soap using goat milk, dried homegrown herbs and flowers and essential oils.

Left: Llama show favorite Spot On. Right: a new mama and her cria.

the country and meeting other breeders.

May 1 Yesterday we set up the stalls with bedding, water and hay, and we hung our stall decorations and signs. We let the llamas rest after being unloaded. Today we showed our appaloosa male, placing fourth in a large, competitive class.

May 2 We showed the younger boys today. The classes were large and the competition was some of the best. Shows are a good way to promote your breeding program and see how your llamas stand up. Our male Spot On RTC was a show favorite; we loved the compliments and interest in his future offspring.

May 3 Weaning day! We brought two female llamas from my parents' farm over to a new pasture to wean their crias. The babies are seven months old and eating grain and green grass.

May 4 Let me describe a typical day on the farm: We get up early and let the chickens and ducks out of the coops. Then we milk the goats. We check all the llamas, and then we're off to our day jobs. We do our main chores in the evening: feeding grain and hay to the llamas and goats, giving fresh water to all the animals, moving chicken tractors (portable chicken coops) to foster the growth of fresh grass, adding feed to each coop, and taking care of the rabbits and ducks. We give the llamas extra attention by rubbing their backs or necks or feeding

them horse treats. They respond by giving us kisses (putting their noses on us).

May 5 We try to maintain a herd of about 20 llamas. As new crias arrive, we decide if any of them will improve our program. We look for correct conformation and fiber characteristics that will make fine wool products. Those we decide not to keep may go to another farm's breeding program or be sold as pets, guard llamas or sources of fiber.

BREEDING TIME & LLAMA BEANS

May 6 Goat milk soap is big in our family because it keeps our skin soft and hydrated. I've been freezing goat milk from our supply, since my mom is ready to make another batch of soap. She adds essential oils and dried herbs and flowers from our gardens. The soap will cure for a few weeks and then be ready to use.

May 7 I updated the website and put together a sales list. The industry is strong and llamas are selling fast. I work with buyers to find the right fit for their program and to make sure the llamas go to good homes.

May 8 We sheared two llamas, leaving three to go. The fleeces were skirted and bagged. Once the entire herd has been shorn, we'll wash the fleeces and grade them. Then we'll group like-colored fleece to send to the mills to get spun into yarn that is all the same color lot.

Stone Crest Llamas, where all hands are happily on deck.

May 9 We breed llamas in the spring and fall to avoid weather that is too cold or too warm. They're stall-bred so we know the exact breeding dates and when to start monitoring the pregnant females more closely. This also helps in case there is an issue during birthing, though that's pretty rare. Today we bred two of the open females that had crias last fall.

May 10 We maintain beautiful perennial gardens on our farms. My mom and I have been spending quite a bit of time pulling weeds, planting new flowers and adding mulch. We also spread "llama beans" in all the flower and vegetable gardens.

May 11 After milking and barn chores, we did a quick pregnancy check of the females we bred on Sunday. Both were spitting on the male. Yep, llamas spit at the male when they're pregnant, so it's a good way to ascertain pregnancy.

May 12 Because of frost, we started covering all the strawberry plants, blueberry bushes and apple trees—which are in full bloom—in hopes of getting fruit later this year.

May 13 We began skirting the wool, which means sorting the fiber by length, fineness and color. We removed the dirt and hay by putting the fleece in a mesh box and using a cattle blower to get the fiber clean. Then we boxed the fiber and shipped it to a mill for processing. Sometimes we hold on to fleeces that we want to process ourselves. For example, I kept the fleece from Spot On, in order to card it, spin it and make it into a shawl or hat that I'll know was from him.

May 14 The fleeces we kept back were washed and laid out to dry. We dyed some of the white fiber to make colorful yarns, then carded the fiber and put it into batts for felting or spinning. My mom and I have wheels and enjoy spinning in winter. My daughter and I also love to felt. She has created many felted pieces that we frame and sell in our store. My son makes needle-felted items to sell.

May 15 It has warmed up, so we tilled the gardens in preparation for planting vegetables. My parents also have a greenhouse full of vegetables and flowers. We use llama manure compost to start all our plants, and we add it to the garden, too, where the tomatoes grow taller than me.

Summer will be a time to enjoy fresh vegetables and fruit from the garden and to watch crias playing in the pastures. We'll fill the barn with hay for winter, and there's always lots of weeding and mowing to do. We'll process much of the fiber into yarn, which will supply our socks, hats, mittens and scarves. We'll dye yarn and roving for our knitting, crocheting and felting customers. And we'll keep busy turning fiber into products to sell in the fall.

THE LONG WAY

Sometimes it is more rewarding to focus
on the journey—not the destination

STEPHANIE BLESER ST. CHARLES, MO

The dry creek bed in front of me is bridged by a fallen tree. The bark is long gone, and what's left of the trunk has been softened by insects and time. Bits of rotten wood fall away and stir up a pungent, earthy smell as I step on the tree, but the center feels strong.

I stretch out my arms for balance and walk steadily across. The creek bank rises to meet me.

I pick a few sticky burrs off my pants and take in the forest around me. Sunlight trickles through the maple and elm trees—still mostly bare. Frost lingers where the sun does not touch. The air is cold and stings my cheeks, but specks of green buds promise warmer days ahead. Hints of burnt coffee and cinnamon mingle with the scent of pine. My father must be having a cigar before leaving.

I could stand here forever, but there is somewhere I must go. I pick my way through the brush, choosing my steps carefully. Dried leaves hide rocks and roots. A squirrel crashes through the undergrowth, its bushy tail trailing behind. A moment later, it darts up a nearby tree and leaps from branch to branch, much like a fearless acrobat on a trapeze.

A glint of bright red catches my eye. Perched near the top of a cedar tree is a cardinal, his fiery feathers bright against dark green needles. I scan the neighboring trees and see his mate, her mostly tan feathers offset by red accents.

I let the rocky creek bed guide me toward my destination. Ahead, under a narrow blacktop road, is a metal tunnel just wide enough for a person to crawl through. I squat down and peer inside. It is dark, but a warm circle of light beckons to me at the other end. Almost there.

Dropping to my knees, I crawl. The air is musty, and I breathe through my mouth to avoid the smell. A car passes overhead, and it thunders louder than a fighter jet at takeoff. I move faster, ignoring the mud seeping through my pants.

I reach the end and scramble into the light. My eyes adjust and take in the lake. It is as still as glass—a mirror of bright blue sky and cedar trees. A tackle box lies open on a wooden picnic table nearby.

"Did you enjoy the long way?" my father asks, handing me a baited fishing rod. The smell of coffee and cinnamon returns.

"I always do."

I cast my line into the lake, and the mirror ripples.

The woods behind Stephanie Bleser's childhood home hold special memories for her.

LONGHORNS & LAND PRESERVATION

A devoted conservationist keeps the bottom line in mind
as he develops his Tennessee farmland

GEORGE LINDEMANN GRANDVIEW, TN

Hi, I'm George Lindemann, the owner of Coal Creek Farm, which is on top of Tennessee's Cumberland Plateau escarpment at about 2,300 feet. I am also a businessman, developer, philanthropist, conservationist and father of a 19-year-old son, a 15-year-old daughter and 13-year-old twins.

Since acquiring this farm, I've learned to appreciate the value of a great controlled burn and rare insects. I manage the farm with new technology and thinking coupled with some of the old ways. In the process, I'm developing ways to feed native grass to my Texas longhorns while encouraging its growth. The grasses have brought back native flora and fauna that declined after years of clear-cutting. I'm also working to have Soak and Piney creeks designated as Wild and Scenic Rivers with expanded public access.

SPRING ON THE PLATEAU
April 1 This morning we rotated cattle toward the soup bowl–shaped pond I dug 15 years ago. Dirt therapy is good for me, and it soothes my soul to see the cattle enjoying it. We migrated the herd to the woods at the top of the property, where they will live for six weeks to two months. Longhorns can sustain themselves in the woods in spring, and their foraging opens the underbrush.

Our ranch manager, Harold, and my oldest son and I loaded tools and headed to the "hayfield" to fix fence. We call this area the hayfield because it was the first place we ever cut hay.

April 2 I got an early start today picking up trash that blew in during the winter. It's incredible how much plastic from the round hay bales' wrapping get caught in the tall grass along the fence line.

April 3 After splitting wood, my kids and I jumped into the ATVs. We stopped to check on the barn cats and our retired mules, Pat and Pam.

Spring is emerging on the farm. The daffodils are outshining the forsythia, and the redbuds are also in bloom. I hope they're not showing off too early, as we expect another freeze next week. Our longhorns live in fields where native grasses (and weeds) sprout. Timing the herd movement just right ensures they'll eat the new growth. The longhorns, in conjunction with controlled burns, are slowly helping us re-create the savannas that existed on the plateau but have been replaced by fescue fields or logging timber.

April 4 Ten healthy longhorn and longhorn-mix calves were born overnight. Since their mothers were tending to them, I focused on other tasks. We bush hogged briars and sedges so these plants won't be a problem when we harvest hay later this season. It costs the same to cut and bail a briar (which the cows don't like) as it does good quality fescue grass. So while it takes time and fuel, in the long run we'll break even and be profitable—with better quality hay.

Flowers are popping up everywhere and the cattle seem to love this weather as much as I do.

Weeding is a constant struggle, especially since our fields were planted on recently clear-cut land. We have spent 15 years reshaping what the loggers left behind, and the fields improve each year. Still, they don't compare to those of our neighbors who have been cutting the same land for nearly 50 years. Reclamation takes time.

April 5 The crew ran out of time with the bush hog yesterday, so we finished the lower field before the rain today. Equipment maintenance was next. Our land has a thick layer of topsoil, so when it rains, we stop running machines over the fields to avoid carving ruts.

Today I saw a bald eagle flying overhead. It reminded me to refill the feeders, since Coal Creek Farm is directly in the

Left: George Lindemann, soaks up the view from his Cumberland Plateau farm. Above: A curious bull investigates a visitor.

Coal Creek Farm houses several large sculptural pieces, such as this one by an artist friend of George's.

migration path for so many birds. In 2020, my kids and I documented about 70 different bird types. We learned the names and calls of so many of them. The short migration season (two to three weeks long) always has us wishing for more time and more birds.

April 6 Our land is divided by Coal Creek and Whites Creek. There is a spot that has gotten worn by ATV crossings, and we often gather rocks by hand and embed them in the steep part of the bank. Most of the major creeks have been fenced so the cows can't access them, but there are many bodies of water on the farm. We carefully maintain all our creek and wet-weather conveyance beds. When the cows gather to drink, it looks lovely and natural, but they leave a mess that leads to soil erosion. They also poop in the water, which carries the waste downstream to areas where people swim. It's critical to stabilize the banks and create as many ponds as possible without interfering with stream flow.

April 7 Today was the perfect day to hike to the top of Bear Den Mountain. It's the highest point on the farm and has a spectacular view that includes Grassy Cove, the Sequatchie Valley (between Cumberland Plateau and Walden's Ridge) and the Tennessee River Valley. Sometimes I can see Great Smoky Mountains National Park, which is about 75 miles away from the farm.

CANOEING & CATTLE

April 8 What should've been just a little rain arrived as snow flurries that persisted as we worked. We're looking for fallen trees so we can repair broken fences and rotate the cows to fresh grass. The herd moved from the soup bowl to the fields by Winter Road. Visitors enjoy seeing cattle graze in this area near the farm's entrance. They drive slowly to watch the calves do their thing.

April 9 Every step I took this morning made a satisfying crunch on the frost underfoot. Returning from my morning hike, I stopped to talk with Harold. He said the shots I heard earlier were related to coyotes getting too close to the herd. I love to hear coyotes sing at night, but we can't let them take our animals.

April 10 Since moving here, I have become an avid whitewater canoer. Canoeing traces back to the Native peoples who farmed this land for centuries. Coal Creek, Whites Creek and Powder Creek flow from my farm down the mountain to the Tennessee River, on to the Ohio, then the Mississippi and into the Gulf of Mexico. These waterways have been crucial to navigation and trade.

April 11 I like to walk around my farm instead of always driving. It's part of a healthy lifestyle that includes exercise, smart eating and mental floss. A cool spring day offers the advantage of no snakes or ticks. The cattle watch me when I'm on foot but run when I'm on a machine. Some have run straight through our fencing, which can injure them and add to my chore list. Walking puts me closer to the wild mammals and birds that have long fascinated me. In addition, the fungi I find in spring are fantastic. They are considered non-timber forest products (NTFP). Wild edible mushrooms could be a profit center if I could figure out how to find enough of them!

April 12 This morning I looked out and saw a beautiful expanse of clouds wrapping the top of the mountain, where my house stands. It's amazing to go from being able to see the Smokies (40 miles across the valley) to barely seeing 30 feet away.

April 13 We raise longhorns and Black Angus. Black Angus meat has good fat content that produces marbling and

The equipment shed holds all manner of farm machinery.

improved flavor compared to other species. But the cattle eat cool-season, non-native grasses only, which are more costly to grow and maintain. Longhorns are very hardy, requiring less water than many other breeds. Although they can look intimidating, they're docile and tend to use their horns (which can reach 5 feet across) to clear underbrush in the woods. This allows them access to fodder that other cows ignore. Even so, I watch them as I work. If they get spooked, those horns can cause major damage. Their meat is leaner than Angus and therefore less desirable. They eat native warm-season grass, some weeds and spring forest growth. We use them to help expand our native grass savannas. Financially it's a toss-up, but I want to bring the ecology back to its native state, so we raise more longhorns than Angus.

BIRDS, BOATS & BURNS

April 15 I enjoy the bright colors, songs and antics of the bird species that pass through our area. Last year a pair of killdeer nested just off the side of our driveway. They feigned injury whenever we passed the nest.

April 17 The kids and I took a kayak outing on Obed River's Clear Creek. This beautiful stretch is the only federally protected waterway in Tennessee. The water quality lives up to its name, and the cliffs that tower overhead seem to stand guard for the river.

April 18 The controlled burn season is short but important for providing wildlife habitat, encouraging the growth of native plants, supplying fodder for the cattle and preventing accidental fires. Today I met with Jacqueline Broeker, the Strike Team coordinator for the state department of ag's forestry division. She will lead the burn crews here. Jacqueline is an experienced burn boss, and I am confident in her leadership and crew.

April 19 I didn't sleep well. Two years ago, while doing a burn, the wind picked up in the evening and our fire threatened to get away from us. I will never forget it. Though the crew contained the blaze, it served as a reminder of how fast a burn can move. It's good to have Jacqueline on our team this time around.

April 20 The weather yesterday cooperated and our burn began as planned. I woke early today, checked in with Jacqueline and rode out with her to ensure the crew was ready.

BIODIVERSITY ON THE FARM

April 22 It's interesting to see newly burned fields in a charred state. Today's inspection showed that even though the fire engulfed the designated areas, some shrubs and trees were unscathed. That's called a patchy burn, which creates a diverse mosaic on the landscape. Some places look barren, but grasses will soon cover these fields. By next season we'll turn cattle out to graze.

From the front porch of the farmhouse, George can admire his longhorns and watch the calves as they romp along the fields, exploring their new world.

April 23 The farm has had a lot of traffic this month, and its miles of gravel roads have paid a high price. Such roads are labor-intensive to maintain, but this is part of the cost of a successful farm. Today was a good day to get on the grader and deal with some of the worst spots.

April 25 As I walked toward the barn, I took a short detour to check the flow of water coming into the upper pond. Adequate water supply is critical for the cattle operation, and protecting water quality is a job I take seriously. Cattle lead healthier lives when they have access to clean water. I like to keep the cattle high on the mountain in spring when the smaller creeks are flowing. They can drink from these sources until June. In summer's heat, our ponds at the lower elevation become their primary source of water.

April 26 I checked on some of the recently burned woods. By clearing underbrush and allowing us to reseed native grasses, these burns help us restore the habitat of the northern bobwhite (aka bobwhite quail), which is facing extinction. I was ecstatic last summer when we managed to capture one on video.

April 28 Flowers are popping up everywhere and the cattle seem to love this weather as much as I do. The calves look fat and happy as they explore farther from their mothers' sides. It makes me smile to watch them run and jump as they charge down the field. We've been breeding our cattle with the goal of creating the perfect bull for the plateau. I'm sure a few of this year's calves will strengthen the herd's genetic lines.

April 29 I love this land. Coal Creek is at the heart of biodiversity in the region. Sure, I've had to make choices. I've had to choose between zombie beetles and poison to save my hemlock trees that were dying from invasive beetles. (Zombie beetles eat the others; poison is just poison.) I've learned to appreciate the value that a natural ecosystem adds to the farm. I watch the bottom line, of course, but I also watch the native grasses and wildlife return. I look forward to seeing what the next 10 years will bring.

April 30 Coal Creek Farm is a cattle farm, an environmental experiment and the catalyst for so many memories. I often recall specific locations—like the spot where my oldest daughter found a special mushroom or where my oldest son photographed a common grackle. Helping the land resemble what it looked like hundreds of years ago is a lifelong task, but I'm up for it. I'm incredibly lucky to live in this paradise while contributing to the local environment and economy.

GENTLE GIANT

From tiny pup to big boy, this dog has always been as sweet as table scraps

KATHY HANEY KINTNERSVILLE, PA

My son, Scott, brought Guss home as a surprise in January 2015. Our adorable new pup was a little ball of fur who soon grew into a 150-plus-pound gentle giant.

While Guss may be slow to get out of bed most mornings, he enjoys himself once he's up. His favorite part of the day is riding out to the farm. He sticks his head out of the car's sunroof or the truck's window, or enjoys the sights from the passenger seat of the four-wheeler. He hates to be left behind and is always up for any adventure with Scott. Guss also patrols the farm for any steers that may have gotten out, and he loudly alerts us to the arrival of visitors.

Guss is truly a part of our family. During the holidays, he eagerly waits for his gifts and opens them all by himself. He's usually more than happy to help others open their gifts as well!

During every meal, Guss positions himself at the table—often with his chin resting on the edge—ready to accept any morsel we're willing to share with him. In the living room, he has his own La-Z-Boy rocking chair. This is the only piece of furniture he's allowed to sit on, and he naps there frequently.

Overall, Guss is a good boy, although at times he can be a bit devilish. More than once, his unrestrained nature has gotten him in trouble, such as when he chased a skunk, thinking it was a cat. Although Guss' size and bark are intimidating to some, he is a very sweet dog and is easily one of our family's best friends.

Scrapbook

CAPTURE THE BEAUTY AROUND YOU

1. KICKING OFF SPRING
I take my daughter to visit the tulip fields every year to welcome the warmer weather and beautiful new blooms.
AMANDA BAILEY AUBURN, WA

2. FARM PLAY
Our son was thrilled to visit Papa and Bama on their farm and meet the new calf. Of course, he always loves "driving" the tractor too.
LEAH KOBES SPOKANE, WA

1. LATE WINTER, EARLY SPRING

It was mid-March—almost the official start of spring, according to the calendar. But in this area, it's usually a mixed bag of weather, including freezing rain. Judging by the look on our guy Frank's face, he's had enough of winter, too!

BRENDA KELLY CHILLICOTHE, IL

2. A MOO-VING PERFORMANCE

On this visit, my daughter, Josie, played violin for the cows. What a neat opportunity to instill enthusiasm for the country in a child!

SARAH COLLINS WALDO, OH

3. STABLE FRIENDS

Our dog Boone protects our horses and goats and has a blast doing it! When the horses eat, he runs around grabbing sticks so he has something to play with and eat too.

JENNIFER DEVITT ORTEGA MOUNTAIN, CA

1. ALL IN THE FAMILY

This image illustrates chore time on our farm. We love that we're able to raise our son here, where he is learning all about hard work and good values.

ELIZABETH McKINNEY ONTARIO, OR

2. STEADY NOW

I often stop at Gilbert's Corner Regional Park in Virginia after work. Walking the trail is so cathartic after a long shift at the hospital. The wildflowers offer an abundant buffet for the birds. I love this photo of a song sparrow because of how it's perched between the two stalks.

LAURA FRAZIER KEARNEYSVILLE, WV

3. A MOTHER'S LOVE

We hosted a neighbor's mare and foal for some months. Watching their interactions and the foal's curiosity and zest for life was a great highlight of those days. Right after I took this photo, she lifted her head to let him pass under and they both went back to grazing.

CANDICE ESTEP LIPAN, TX

3

ROAD LESS TRAVELED

If you travel the back roads of East
Texas in springtime, you will see
large wisteria vines that cover every
hill and dale. Wisteria in full bloom
is flush with beautiful lavender
cascading blossoms that sometimes
stretch from tree to tree over the
county roads. I happened upon one
such road while exploring the
countryside near Tyler, Texas. The
light at the end of the road seemed
to beckon me to places beyond.

LINDA DAVIDSON TYLER, TX

1. MEET CUTE
I offered to take some photographs of my neighbors' baby goat and brought my dog, Murphy, along. He was curious and wanted to get a closer look!

BIRGIT DAVIDSON LA LUZ, NM

2. IS SHE BACK YET?
I saw three young pileated woodpeckers at Brazos Bend State Park in Texas one spring. They stuck their heads out of the tree, waiting for their mother to feed them.

JEFFREY ZWIERS KATY, TX

3. GIRL POWER
My granddaughter Charlea enjoys farm chores. She's still small, but she's a great helper. She assists in scooping manure from the donkey barn, getting feed for the animals and operating the well pump to get water for the garden.

TAMMY WILLIAMS MADISON, MO

1. TEA TIME

On our dairy farm we have cows, donkeys, chickens, ducks, goats, alpacas, sheep, dogs and cats. But my daughter Lilly bonded with this particular chicken, Millie, right from the start. Millie is full-grown now and she always runs to Lilly first when we're all outside.

REBECCA BALLINGER JEFFERSON CITY, TN

2. THIS LITTLE PIGGY LOVES FUN

My mini pig Oliver and his brother, Henry, live at a horse stable in nearby Orange Park Acres. Oliver is 2 years old, and his favorite things include playing chase, belly rubs, new toys and tomatoes.

ASHLEE DuCOING NEWPORT BEACH, CA

3. SPRING SHOW

It was an unexpected surprise to have a yellow warbler visit our flowering pear tree. The bird arrived on an unseasonably cold morning in early May. Its little body was puffed out for warmth and its tiny head was lifted skyward, which made it look all the more sweet.

PAT SHAW WARREN, MI

1. HERE FOR THE TREATS

Our pigs, Ginger and MaryAnn, will follow me anywhere—as long as I have crackers to share.

BEVERLY FRANKENY SEVEN STARS, PA

2. FUTURE SOIL SCIENTIST

My daughter Amaryllis is a bright young lady who loves to feed the chickens and gather their eggs, collect bugs and smell any and all flowers. Playing in the dirt is arguably her favorite pastime.

ANDREA HANCHEY VALLEY SPRINGS, CA

3. TINY PRANCER

Nod may be a bit smaller than his siblings, Wynken and Blynken, but he's a total sweetheart!

CAROL ANDERSEN WALTON, NE

1. PRECIOUS CARGO
After our American Mastiff, Deeks, hopped up into this wagon, our oldest son, Hank, gave it his all to take his best buddy for a ride.

AMELIA HESS JEFFERSON, OR

2. LOOK OUT BELOW
Mama called this wood duck chick to jump out of the nest just one day after it hatched. I have three nest boxes, each with a security camera inside so I'll know when this event will happen. The chicks had no flight feathers yet, so they bounced, rolled and plopped to the ground before joining their mom. It was adorable to watch.

SUE CLARK STUART, FL

3. WINNING SMILE
My son Nixon showed his first calf ever at the county fair, and he took first place. He was so proud of his trophy, just like the ones his older brothers have. Long after the fair, we still love to take the calf on walks.

KIM LUNDGREN WEST UNION, IA

Heart & Soul

Tina and Brion live on a farm on the outskirts of Brenham, Texas, with two rescue dogs.

SIMPLY TINA

A barrel racer, writer and philanthropist, Tina Webb
is proof that good things come to those who wait

JILL GLEESON APPALACHIAN MOUNTAINS, PA

Tina Webb describes her farm as a slice of heaven. The property, which she inherited from her grandfather, sits on 13 rolling acres in Texas, between Austin and Houston. Pecan trees planted generations ago surround the house she lives in with her husband, Brion Webb, a retired United Airlines pilot. Two dogs, both rescues, roam free, while four quarter horses bunk in the barn. The open arena where she practices barrel riding is farther out back, and neighbors—friendly as they may be—are few and far between. It's quiet and serene, the perfect place for an author to work on her next book.

When she isn't writing or riding, Tina sometimes invites ladies from the Cowboy Church of Brenham, Texas, to join her for group Bible study. She says their visits bring her life "more joy and peace," as well as patience, which is not a quality that has always come easily to her. A self-described "doer and goer," Tina says that when she decides she wants to do something, she does it 110 percent. "For me to have an idea and then wait, or be patient, is not really in my being," she admits. But she also believes that "if it's in God's timing and you do wait, the end result is better than you could have ever done yourself."

Tina took up barrel racing shortly before turning 50.

Tina has certainly taken her time exploring two of her life's greatest passions, and she's a living reminder that sometimes success doesn't come immediately. She's now widely known as both an author and a barrel racer, but she had it in her mind to write for more than a decade before she published her first title, a cookbook called *Simply Southern*.

And racing? As a kid growing up on a small farm on the outskirts of Brenham, Texas, she was interested in riding but didn't have many opportunities to saddle up until her parents bought her a horse, an 18-year-old Appaloosa, when she was about 9 years old.

DREAM ON

"We didn't have the funds for barrel racing—the kind of horse I'd need, the trailer, the money for competitions—so I would take my old horse and pretend to run barrels," Tina recalls, remembering that she had to create fake barrels because she couldn't get her hands on real ones.

Tina began working part time during her high school years, and she let her hobby fall by the wayside for quite a while. Eventually she married her first husband and they had two children together, Claire Reue Bretischopf and Colin Reue. She dedicated the next two decades of her life to raising them, but she never fell out of love with the idea of racing. And once her kids were both in college, when she was just short of 50 years old, she returned to her first love.

Nowadays she spends most weekends riding throughout the Lone Star State, often in Southeast Texas Barrel Racing Association events. But when she has the time, she occasionally makes forays into Oklahoma and Louisiana for competitions. She's had a lot of success, too, winning belt buckles, cash prizes and even a saddle.

"If I can spend a day with my horse," she says, "something about that just brings me so much joy." She's drawn to the sheer thrill of the competition, which takes both great skill and nerve, and to the people she encounters on the rodeo circuit. "I've made great friends," she says, adding that she's always been appreciative of their dedicated and upbeat attitudes. "I really enjoy the entire experience."

THE WRITE STUFF

Tina loves writing every bit as much as she loves the rodeo. *Simply Southern*, which came out in 2018, is a gorgeous coffee-table-sized cookbook filled with mouthwatering recipes that run alongside bright, bold photographs. Family and faith have always been important to Tina, and both are featured prominently on the cover of the book, which showcases a long, simply laid table that's set outside against the backdrop of a rustic church.

Tina shares some of her favorite Bible verses inside the cookbook, but she leaves plenty of room for the recipes themselves too. Among the standouts are a hearty chicken tortilla soup, a dewberry crunch dessert (featuring a filling made with the fruit, which grows wild in Texas), and a dressing that Tina's grandmother used to whip up each year for Thanksgiving.

"For the most part, the recipes are very southern, and very simple," Tina explains. "They're handed-down recipes that have been in our family for generations. I love to cook and to bake because it reminds me of my mother and my grandmother, and I just love serving people through food. I think this book is about the generations. It's about the memories."

GIVING BACK

Tina has also found a way to serve through her writing. She donates a portion of the sales that she receives from *Simply Southern* to the Adam's Angels Ministry, a charity founded by close friends of Tina's whose young son was diagnosed with leukemia. The group provides emotional, financial and also spiritual support to young cancer patients and their families. And some of the income she receives from her second book, *Harvey Gets Rescued*—which tells the story of how

And I just love serving people through food.

Tina and Brion came to adopt one of their beloved dogs—benefits shelters that care for homeless animals.

Currently working in sales while also helping with the marketing for a friend's new landscape supply company, Tina plans to keep barrel racing. She might even find the time to try her hand again at mounted shooting, which she and Brion used to compete in together. She's also been working on another book, a devotional, though she's not sure yet when it might come out. Still, she is sure that she'll continue to find joy in her family and in the land on which she lives.

Tina says that her parents taught her the importance of family early on in her life. "And of course we did a lot outside," she says, thinking back on her childhood on the farm. "I had my horse. We had dogs. I think that influenced me. I like living a quiet life. I look at the sky, the stars and the rolling hills, just the beauty of what God has created, and I feel so fortunate to live here and be around people who love and help each other."

Tina loves baking, in large part because it reminds her of time spent in the kitchen with her mother and grandmother.

Minnie and Mr. Fluffy became fast friends.

MINNIE THE MOOCHER

Life lessons learned from a stray cat

CAREN RAMON LA VERNIA, TX

It is said that during the Great Depression, itinerant workers would mark the gates of houses where they were welcomed with a sandwich or a meal. I believe stray cats have done the same thing to my home.

Over the last 25 years, about a dozen have appeared on my porch, gazing through the glass door. Even as my husband said, "Don't feed that cat, Caren," I opened the door, cat food in hand.

Most of the cats stayed only a few days before disappearing into the woods by our house. Except for one. She stayed 11 years.

MEETING MINNIE

One evening, I was stewing over a hurtful remark a woman at church had made. Replaying it in my mind, I caught a glimpse of a black tail underneath our tack shed. Later, after our two cats had eaten, a skinny, scraggly young tabby crept up and finished their leftovers.

Soon she was showing up daily for dinner. I named her Minnie the Moocher. It was obvious she was feral. I doled out food just for her, but she'd always shy away while I scooped out her share.

Minnie stuck around, dividing her time between our tack shed and the porch. She was no longer scrawny, and I congratulated myself on her new health. However, she kept gaining weight—especially around her middle. She was pregnant.

We fixed up a box in the garage where she could sleep. She knew right away it was for her, and one day I found her there, nursing five kittens.

Once the kittens had all found homes, we decided to have Minnie spayed. When we released her back into our yard, I figured she'd never return. But come suppertime, she was back. Incredibly, she forgave me.

LEARNING TO FORGIVE

It had now been a few months since I'd spoken with the woman from church, but I couldn't stop obsessing over her rude comment. *Dear Lord,* I prayed, *if this cat can forgive me for kidnapping her, surely I can forgive a single insensitive remark. Help me.* From then on, if that upsetting conversation popped into my mind, I made an effort to think of something else.

It was obvious that Minnie missed her kittens and craved affection. Thinking this would be a good time to tame her, I spent hours on the porch, sitting with a bowl of canned cat food next to me. She would sit about 5 feet from me, scrutinizing my every move. I ignored her, reading my book, silently pleading with her to come closer. I finally accepted she was never going to let me touch her, but she became my constant companion. Whenever I'd go outside, she'd meow hello and then follow me around the property. Here was another lesson learned: acceptance.

After a church event one day, I was cleaning up with the aforementioned woman when I decided to apply Minnie's acceptance lesson. I picked up a casserole dish and remarked, "That macaroni and cheese was the best I've ever eaten."

Raising an eyebrow, her eyes boring into mine, she challenged, "That was mine."

"Really? Will you share your recipe?"

She stared at me a moment, allowing her mouth to twist into an almost-smile, and said, "I'll email it to you."

MAKING NEW FRIENDS

One day, I was outside reading while Minnie was curled up in a nearby chair. She bolted up, staring at a large, fluffy ginger tomcat standing on the woods' edge. He came closer, staring at me, ignoring her. Minnie walked up and head-butted him. Startled, he rushed straight to me, hopped into my lap and curled up, purring.

The next day, he was back. Minnie approached again, this time putting her nose to his. He gave her a sniff, then brushed by on his way to my lap. This went on for several days, with Minnie never giving up on winning his friendship. The cat finally caved, giving in to her affectionate rubs.

I was beginning to wonder whose cat this was. I figured that he must belong to a neighbor. But as the days went on, he got skinnier and started following me to the house, begging for food. It was obvious he'd been someone's baby, as it seemed his one goal in life was to be a lap cat.

I scoured the papers for a lost cat listing. I bought a collar and typed up a note with my number and name: "If this is your cat, please call me. I would like to adopt him, but I don't want to steal someone's cat."

A week later, he appeared with scratches all over his face, the collar missing and one ear hanging by a few tendons. In addition to treating his wounds, the vet scanned him for a microchip. Finding none, we adopted him, christening him Mr. Fluffy.

We kept Mr. Fluffy in the house at night to avoid more misadventures and vet bills. But every morning, Minnie was on the porch waiting for him. They ate every meal together and then walked off, the picture of an old married couple.

SAYING GOODBYE

One day, Minnie vanished. Mr. Fluffy and I scoured the property, but we never found her body or any indication of what might have happened. For a while, poor Mr. Fluffy would go out every morning and walk around the house, searching for her before asking to be let back inside.

It always hurts to lose an animal you love, but I wouldn't give up the time we had with Minnie for anything. Feral as she was, she taught me that friendship and love can be shared just by being present and accepting.

Thanks, Minnie, and Godspeed.

Caren Ramon shares her Texas home with her husband and her pets.

If this cat can forgive me for kidnapping her, surely I can forgive a single insensitive remark.

FARM GIRL POWER

Thanks to fortitude and physics, she accomplished the seemingly impossible

MARY KOEBERL RECHENBERG JACKSON, MO

Sons are considered a big asset to a farm couple trying to manage a multitude of chores. But my mama and daddy, Ruby and Joe Kranawetter, had four daughters and no sons on the farm where I grew up, in Cape Girardeau County, Missouri. I was kid number three, born in 1947. At a young age, I realized there is no getting out of work if you live on a farm, and I figured out that I favored outdoor and barnyard jobs over indoor and gardening jobs.

Plenty of chores filled our days. Helping Mama do laundry, dusting and sweeping, carrying in firewood, gathering eggs, weeding the garden, canning hundreds of jars of vegetables and fruits, and many more jobs were delegated to us kids. As soon as you were big enough to carry a few sticks of firewood and dry the dishes without breaking too many, you were ready to join the family workforce.

I made a point of following my daddy around, trying to make myself useful. I'd hand him tools, help doctor a sick calf, and change the sacks when we were grinding feed. It was exciting and didn't feel like work to me. I'm sure Daddy tired of my questions, but we became quite a team.

I loved riding on the fender of the Oliver 70 or the red-belly Ford, and eventually Daddy taught me to drive both. I couldn't wait for hay-hauling time, when a tractor driver was needed to unload bales. By the time I turned 12, Daddy had taught me to rake hay into long, thick windrows ahead of the baler and to disk the freshly plowed fields at planting time.

Left: Mary (bottom right) stands for a photo with her family in front of their farmhouse.
Right: Mary sits for a photo in the family's front yard, just before leaving for college.

Back in the 1950s and '60s we did things in a simpler way. And since Daddy didn't have a hired hand, he found clever ways to do "two-man" jobs. One such job was changing the tractor wheels when the job at hand required a wider or narrower space between them. Straddling two rows of corn was pretty tricky at cultivation time unless the tractor wheels had been spread to the maximum. So Daddy had to remove the lug nuts from each back wheel, pull the wheel off the axle, turn it around and refasten the lug nuts. He didn't have a big fancy jack to lift the tractor.

When I was 10 or 11 years old, I had been hanging around the barn pestering him and watching him prepare equipment for fieldwork when I noticed that he'd started loosening the lug nuts on the back wheels of the Ford. Curious by nature and aware that the tires weren't flat, I had a barrage of questions. For one, I didn't understand how turning the wheels around would widen the distance between them. Daddy explained that the rim of each wheel was designed so that the tire would be a different distance from the center of the tractor depending on which side faced out.

He set up a block of wood that reminded me of a tree stump and a thick board that looked very heavy, pushing the block up near the back of the tractor and placing the board on top of it, with one end up under the axle. He pushed down on parts of the board until he found the spot that allowed him to lift that side of the tractor. This looked a lot like something I had studied in science class, called a lever.

To my surprise, Daddy instructed me to sit on the board at that spot. "Sit still!" he cautioned as I hopped up. Pulling the wheel away from the axle, he turned it around as quickly as he could. It dawned on me that my weight was holding that side of the tractor up, and I sat so still that I barely breathed. I wondered, *How could a little girl like me hold up one side of a tractor?* After all, I weighed only 85 pounds. Within minutes, my daddy had the wheel back in place and we went to the other side to repeat the process. I felt like Superwoman.

At the supper table, Mama asked Daddy about his day. As the conversation came around to the tractor wheels, she asked how he'd managed by himself. He winked

Mary's father, Joe, plants corn with the Ford tractor.

at me and said, "My partner helped me."

I couldn't help bragging to my sisters and a few school friends that I could lift a tractor by myself. Of course, they thought I was full of hot air. Even after I told them how it worked, they eyed me skeptically. I was surprised my sisters didn't want to try it, too, but they'd never had much interest in farmwork.

Years later, while teaching simple machines to my elementary school students, I told the story about the little girl lifting a tractor. My students didn't believe such a feat was possible. I explained it was a lot like riding a seesaw. How I wished I could give them a solid demonstration—or better yet, that I had a picture of myself sitting on that heavy board so long ago. I don't know that I ever convinced them my story was true.

Daddy was a good teacher, never raising his voice or getting mad if I messed up. Helping on the farm created a strong bond between us, and he had a way of making me feel good about myself. He never said, "This is man's work. Go help your mother." I learned a great deal from him that made me a stronger person. He taught me to be resourceful, to be willing to meet a challenge and to find satisfaction in doing my best. It wasn't the tractor-lifting adventure that gave me my superpowers, even though I felt pretty powerful at the time. I've come to realize that thanks to Daddy's love and guidance and the grace of God, I have had the strength and will to do almost anything I set my mind to.

Taste of the Country

ROAST LEG OF LAMB

PREP 5 min. **BAKE** 2 hours + standing
MAKES 10 servings

- 1 bone-in leg of lamb (6 to 8 lbs.), trimmed
- 2 garlic cloves, minced
- ½ tsp. dried thyme
- ½ tsp. dried marjoram
- ½ tsp. dried oregano
- ¼ tsp. salt
- ⅛ tsp. pepper
- 1 tsp. canola oil

1. Preheat oven to 325°. Place lamb on a rack in a shallow roasting pan, fat side up. Cut 12-14 slits ½ in. deep in roast. Combine garlic, thyme, marjoram, oregano, salt and pepper; spoon 2 tsp. into the slits. Brush roast with oil; rub with remaining herb mixture.
2. Bake, uncovered, until meat reaches desired doneness (for medium-rare, thermometer should read 135°; medium, 140°; medium-well, 145°), 2-2½ hours. Let roast stand 15 minutes before slicing.

5 OZ. COOKED LAMB 227 cal., 9g fat (4g sat. fat), 122mg chol., 114mg sod., 0 carb. (0 sugars, 0 fiber), 34g pro.

CHILLED ASPARAGUS WITH BASIL CREAM

TAKES 20 min. **MAKES** 8 servings

- 2 lbs. fresh asparagus, trimmed
- 1 cup mayonnaise
- ¼ cup heavy whipping cream
- 4 Tbsp. minced fresh basil, divided
- 2 fresh garlic cloves, peeled and halved
- ½ tsp. salt
- ¼ tsp. pepper
- 2 Tbsp. pine nuts, toasted
- 1 Tbsp. grated lemon peel

1. In a large saucepan, boil 8 cups water. Add half the asparagus; cook, uncovered, just until crisp-tender, 2-4 minutes. Remove and immediately drop into ice water. Drain and pat dry. Repeat with the remaining asparagus. Arrange on a serving platter.
2. Place mayonnaise, cream, 3 Tbsp. basil, garlic, salt and pepper in a food processor; cover and process until blended. Spoon over asparagus or serve on side. Garnish with pine nuts, lemon peel and remaining 1 Tbsp. basil.

1 SERVING 235 cal., 24g fat (5g sat. fat), 10mg chol., 296mg sod., 3g carb. (1g sugars, 1g fiber), 2g pro.

LEMON RISOTTO WITH BROCCOLI

PREP 25 min. **COOK** 30 min.
MAKES 8 servings

- 3 cans (14½ oz. each) reduced-sodium chicken broth
- 1 Tbsp. olive oil
- 1 small onion, finely chopped
- 1½ cups uncooked arborio rice
- 2 tsp. grated lemon zest
- ½ cup dry white wine or additional reduced-sodium chicken broth
- 3 cups chopped fresh broccoli
- ⅓ cup grated Parmesan cheese
- 1 Tbsp. lemon juice
- 2 tsp. minced fresh thyme

1. In a large saucepan, bring broth to a simmer; keep hot. In another large saucepan, heat oil over medium heat. Add the onion; cook and stir until tender, 3-5 minutes. Add rice and lemon zest; cook and stir until rice is coated, 1-2 minutes.
2. Stir in white wine. Reduce heat to maintain a simmer; cook and stir until wine is absorbed. Add hot broth, ½ cup at a time, cooking and stirring until broth is absorbed after each addition, adding broccoli after half the broth has been added. Cook until rice is tender but firm to the bite and risotto is creamy. Remove from heat; stir in cheese and lemon juice. Sprinkle with thyme.

⅔ CUP 201 cal., 3g fat (1g sat. fat), 3mg chol., 460mg sod., 35g carb. (2g sugars, 2g fiber), 7g pro.

HAM SPREAD

PREP 15 min. + chilling MAKES 2½ cups

- 1 pkg. (8 oz.) cream cheese, softened
- ¼ cup mayonnaise
- ¼ cup ranch salad dressing
- 2 Tbsp. minced fresh parsley
- 1 tsp. finely chopped onion
- ½ tsp. ground mustard
- ½ tsp. hot pepper sauce, optional
- 2 cups finely chopped fully cooked ham
- ⅓ cup chopped pecans
  Assorted crackers

1. In a small mixing bowl, combine the cream cheese, mayonnaise, salad dressing, parsley, onion, mustard and, if desired, pepper sauce until smooth. Stir in the ham. (Mixture will be soft.) Line a 3-cup bowl with plastic wrap. Spoon ham mixture into bowl; cover and refrigerate at least 8 hours or overnight.

2. Invert ham mixture onto a serving plate; remove and discard plastic wrap. Press pecans onto surface of ham mixture. Serve with crackers.

2 TBSP. 100 cal., 9g fat (3g sat. fat), 20mg chol., 248mg sod., 1g carb. (1g sugars, 0 fiber), 4g pro.

LIMONCELLO TIRAMISU

PREP 30 min. + chilling
MAKES 16 servings

- ½ cup sugar
- ¼ cup water
- 2 Tbsp. limoncello

LEMON CURD
- 1½ cups sugar
- ⅓ cup plus 1 Tbsp. cornstarch
- 1½ cups cold water
- 3 large egg yolks, lightly beaten
- 3 Tbsp. butter, cubed
- ½ cup lemon juice
- 2 tsp. grated lemon zest

CREAM FILLING
- 1½ cups heavy whipping cream
- ¾ cup sugar
- 1 carton (8 oz.) mascarpone cheese

ASSEMBLY
- 3 pkg. (3 oz. each) ladyfingers, split
- 4 macaroon cookies, crumbled
  Candied lemon peel, optional

1. In a saucepan, bring sugar and water to a boil. Cook and stir until sugar dissolves. Remove from the heat. Stir in limoncello; set aside.

2. To make the lemon curd, in another saucepan, combine sugar and cornstarch. Stir in water until smooth. Bring to a boil; cook and stir until thickened, about 1 minute. Remove from heat.

3. Stir a small amount of hot mixture into egg yolks; return all to the pan, stirring constantly. Bring to a gentle boil; cook and stir 2 minutes longer. Remove from heat. Stir in butter. Gently stir in lemon juice and zest. Cool to room temperature without additional stirring.

4. In a large bowl, beat cream until it begins to thicken. Add sugar; beat until stiff peaks form. Fold mascarpone cheese and whipped cream into lemon curd.

5. On the bottom of a 9-in. springform pan, arrange a third of the ladyfingers. Drizzle with a third of the syrup; spread with a third of the filling. Repeat layers twice. Cover and refrigerate overnight. Carefully run knife around edge of pan to loosen. Remove sides of pan. Sprinkle with crumbled cookies and, if desired, candied lemon peel.

1 PIECE 396 cal., 20g fat (11g sat. fat), 128mg chol., 57mg sod., 51g carb. (37g sugars, 0 fiber), 4g pro.

EASTER MERINGUE CUPS

PREP 25 min. + standing
BAKE 45 min. + cooling
MAKES 8 servings

3	large egg whites
½	tsp. vanilla extract
¼	tsp. cream of tartar
¾	cup sugar
½	cup lemon curd
1	cup sliced fresh strawberries
2	medium kiwifruit, peeled and sliced
½	cup fresh raspberries
⅓	cup mandarin oranges
⅓	cup cubed fresh pineapple

1. Preheat oven to 275°. Place egg whites in a large bowl; let stand at room temperature for 30 minutes.

2. Beat the egg whites, vanilla and cream of tartar on medium speed until soft peaks form. Gradually beat in sugar, 1 Tbsp. at a time, on high setting until stiff peaks begin to form.

3. Drop meringue into 8 mounds on a parchment-lined baking sheet. Shape into 3-in. cups with the back of a spoon.

4. Bake meringues until set and dry, 45-50 minutes. Turn off oven and do not open door; leave meringues in oven for 1 hour. After removing the meringues from the oven, spread each cup with lemon curd and fill with the fresh fruit mixture.

1 SERVING 180 cal., 1g fat (1g sat. fat), 15mg chol., 38mg sod., 40g carb. (37g sugars, 2g fiber), 2g pro.

BUNNY CAKE

PREP 2 hours **BAKE** 30 min. + cooling
MAKES 20 servings

- ¼ cup sugar
- 2 tsp. cornstarch
- ⅛ tsp. salt
- ½ cup orange juice
- 2 large egg yolks, beaten
- 1 Tbsp. unsalted butter
- 1 tsp. grated orange zest

CAKE
- ½ cup unsalted butter, softened
- 1½ cups sugar
- 4 large egg whites, room temperature
- 2 tsp. clear vanilla extract
- 2 tsp. grated orange zest
- 2¼ cups cake flour
- 1 Tbsp. baking powder
- ½ tsp. salt
- 1 cup 2% milk

BUTTERCREAM
- 3 oz. white baking chocolate, chopped
- 2 Tbsp. heavy whipping cream
- 3 large egg whites, room temperature
- ¾ cup sugar
- ¼ tsp. cream of tartar
- ¼ tsp. salt
- 1 cup unsalted butter, cubed
- 1 tsp. clear vanilla extract
- 1 cup coarse sugar
  Optional bunny decorations: Bright white candy coating, light cocoa candy coating, pink coarse sugar, sprinkles, white paste food coloring, red food coloring, jelly beans

1. To prepare orange curd for cake, in saucepan, combine sugar, cornstarch and salt. Stir in juice until smooth. Bring to a boil; cook and stir 1 minute or until thick.

Remove from heat. Stir small amount of hot mixture into egg yolks; return all to pan, stirring constantly. Bring to a gentle boil; cook and stir 1 minute longer. Remove from heat; gently stir in butter and orange zest. Cool to room temperature without stirring. Refrigerate 1 hour.

2. Preheat oven to 350°. Line three 6-in. round baking pans with parchment; grease pans.

3. Cream butter and sugar until light and fluffy, 5-7 minutes. Add egg whites, 1 at a time, beating well after each. Beat in vanilla and zest. Combine flour, baking powder and salt; add to creamed mixture alternately with the milk.

4. Transfer batter to the prepared pans. Bake until toothpick inserted into the center comes out clean, 30-35 minutes. Cool cakes in pans 10 minutes. Remove to wire racks; remove parchment. Cool completely.

5. Meanwhile, prepare the buttercream by microwaving white chocolate and cream in microwave-safe bowl until melted, stirring every 30 seconds until smooth. Cool slightly. In heatproof bowl of stand mixer, whisk egg whites, sugar, cream of tartar and salt until blended. Place bowl over simmering water in saucepan over medium heat. Whisking mixture constantly, heat until thermometer reads 160°, 5-7 minutes.

6. Remove from heat. With whisk attachment of stand mixer, beat on high speed until cooled to 90°, about 5 minutes. Gradually beat in butter, a few tablespoons at a time, on medium speed until smooth; beat in vanilla and white chocolate mixture.

7. Spread curd between cake layers. Spread buttercream over top and sides of cake; sprinkle coarse sugar over top and sides of cake. If desired, decorate cake to look like a bunny. Store in refrigerator until ready to serve.

1 PIECE 479 cal., 28g fat (17g sat. fat), 93mg chol., 261mg sod., 55g carb. (42g sugars, 0 fiber), 5g pro.

ROSE AND RASPBERRY FOOL

PREP 15 min. + chilling
MAKES 8 servings

- 2 cups fresh or frozen raspberries
- 6 Tbsp. sugar, divided
- 1½ cups heavy whipping cream
- 1 tsp. rose water
  Fresh mint leaves

1. In a small bowl, lightly crush raspberries and 2 Tbsp. sugar. Cover and refrigerate 1-2 hours.
2. In a large bowl, beat cream until it begins to thicken. Add remaining 4 Tbsp. sugar and rose water; beat until soft peaks form. Gently fold in raspberry mixture. Spoon into individual dishes. Garnish dessert with mint leaves and, if desired, additional raspberries. Serve immediately.

½ CUP 206 cal., 16g fat (10g sat. fat), 51mg chol., 13mg sod., 14g carb. (12g sugars, 2g fiber), 2g pro.

FOCACCIA

PREP 30 min. + rising
BAKE 15 min. **MAKES** 2 dozen

- 1 pkg. (¼ oz.) active dry yeast
- 1¼ cups warm water (110° to 115°), divided
- 1 Tbsp. honey
- 3 cups all-purpose flour
- ¼ cup plus 3 Tbsp. olive oil, divided
- ¾ tsp. kosher salt
- 1 tsp. flaky sea salt, optional
  Assorted vegetables, optional

1. In a large bowl, dissolve the yeast in ½ cup warm water and honey; let stand for 5 minutes. Add flour, ¼ cup oil, salt and remaining ¾ cup water; mix until smooth (dough will be wet). Scrape sides of bowl clean; cover and let rise in a warm place until doubled, about 45 minutes.
2. Preheat oven to 425°. Brush a 13x9-in. baking dish or 12-in. cast-iron skillet with 1 Tbsp. oil. Gently scrape dough directly into pan. With oiled hands, gently spread to fill pan. If dough springs back, wait 10 minutes and stretch again. Make indentations in dough with fingers. Drizzle with 2 Tbsp. oil; let rise until doubled in size, 30-40 minutes.
3. If desired, sprinkle with sea salt and decorate with vegetables. Bake until golden brown, 20-25 minutes. Serve warm.

1 PIECE 95 cal., 4g fat (1g sat. fat), 0 chol., 61mg sod., 13g carb. (1g sugars, 1g fiber), 2g pro.

Handcrafted

BUNNY WREATH

WHAT YOU'LL NEED

Grapevine wreaths
(1 large, 1 medium, 2 small)
Floral wire
Stems of pussy willow
Ribbon
Wire cutters
Hot glue gun

DIRECTIONS

1. Attach the medium wreath to the top of the large wreath with floral wire. These pieces will become the head and body of the bunny.

2. Compress each of the small wreaths in the middle to create an oval shape. The ends will snap just a little, and the oval shape should hold.

3. Attach the small oval wreaths to the medium wreath with floral wire to create the ears.

4. Snip some stems from the willow branches and weave them into the wreaths.

5. Loop a bow tightly around the bunny's neck with ribbon. Use hot glue to secure it.

6. Hang the wreath from the back of the ribbon.

GARDEN VARIETY

WHAT YOU'LL NEED

Chair spindles
Orange, maroon and white paint
Foliage floral picks
Saw
Paintbrush
Drill or hot glue gun

DIRECTIONS

1. Use a saw to cut down several mismatched chair spindles to the desired lengths.
2. Paint them to look like carrots, radishes and parsnips.
3. Drill a hole into the top of each spindle and push a few sprigs of artificial greenery into it, or use hot glue to attach the greens to the top of each spindle.

CHIME TIME

WHAT YOU'LL NEED

Ribbons
8-in. embroidery hoop
Large beads
Skeleton keys
Twine
Key ring

DIRECTIONS

1. Wrap ribbons around hoop and tie, allowing the ends of varying lengths to hang below.
2. Thread large beads onto some of the ribbons and secure them by knotting underneath.
3. Tie skeleton keys to the ends of half of the ribbons, varying their height.
4. Cut two 18-in. pieces of twine. Tie the ends of the first piece to opposite points on the hoop. Repeat the process with the second piece so that the pieces are perpendicular.
5. Loop key ring around the twine where the lengths intersect and use to hang the wind chime.

Summer

As day breaks over the Cascade Range in Oregon, an early riser cuts through calm waters on a mirrored lake.

PHOTO BY RON AND PATTY THOMAS/ GETTY IMAGES

The Good Life

FROM THE GROUND UP

Gardener Ashlie Thomas believes that everyone deserves access to fresh, nourishing food

ASHLEY ABRAMSON MILWAUKEE, WI

Ashlie Thomas grew up in the rural South and knows firsthand what it's like to live in a food desert. She also knows that food insecurity can be a problem even in communities with plenty of restaurants and grocery stores. "When we think of food insecurity, we usually think about food deserts, but many people live in food swamps, where there's an oversaturation of fast food," she says. "I've experienced both ends of the spectrum."

Ashlie, now in her early 30s, developed an interest in nutrition in 2015 when she started taking care of her grandfather, who was ill. She learned how hard it could be to keep her grandparents' kitchen stocked with the nourishing produce they needed to keep themselves healthy.

The answer to her community's problem turned out to be right in front of her, in the lush North Carolina soil. "I was so motivated and encouraged by the land," she says, "and how it could be used to grow nutritious foods."

In 2019, Ashlie and her husband, Tyler Thomas, bought a home on an acre of land in Graham, North Carolina. Shortly after moving in, she and Tyler, who both work full-time jobs outside the home, built several octagonal raised beds on their property. Three years later, they have 2,500 square feet of organic gardens where they grow up to 70 types of fruits, vegetables and herbs per season.

When she isn't working in her garden, Ashlie spends time online. Through her platform, The Mocha Gardener, she educates her 20,000 followers about nutrition, food insecurity and gardening. Her goal? To empower people to improve their health by cultivating gardens of their own.

On her Instagram, Facebook and YouTube accounts, Ashlie shares tips for gardening and affordable meal planning. She's also working on a book about gardening and nutrition.

Ashlie is a firm believer that you don't need to have an acre of land, or even a backyard, to reap your own edible harvest, and she wants to make gardening as accessible as possible for her followers.

"You might not have a farm, and you don't have to grow for the masses," she says, "but you can grow for yourself and your family even with limited space."

Along with making it easier to eat nutritious foods, Ashlie believes that teaching people how to create and tend to their own gardens can boost their health in other important ways: The hard work of planting and digging up soil, for example, is excellent exercise. And spending time outside in a garden can promote mental health too. It's always encouraging to see a process through from start to finish and, she says, there's something special about getting your hands dirty. Studies suggest that the act of touching soil can be soothing to the mind as well as the body—it offers a simple but effective way to slow down and reconnect with nature.

Reflecting on her story so far, Ashlie says she couldn't have imagined the ways her garden and her message would thrive. "That's the beauty in this whole journey," she says. "We plant the seed, we nurture it, and we leave space for it to do its impactful work—not just for us but for those around us."

Ashlie has been planting and growing vegetables at her North Carolina home since 2019.

Kyle and Tressa Graveley operate a ranch with the help of their three children: Kadin, Reid and Natalie.

THREE GENERATIONS UNDER ONE BIG SKY

Grazing and grizzlies come with the territory on this family-operated Montana ranch

TRESSA GRAVELEY HELMVILLE, MT

Hi there! I'm Tressa Graveley. My life on a Montana ranch dates back to the summer road construction job I took in 2003, when a rancher named Kyle (who regularly drove through my job site) came to be the first in a line of halted traffic. Kyle teases that I pursued him because I stopped him every day, whereas he was only following traffic rules. At any rate, here we are: married and living on his family's ranch with our kids, Kadin, Natalie and Reid (14, 12 and 6).

The main ranch, established in 1867, is where Kyle's mom and dad, Steve and Sue Graveley, live, as do his sister and brother-in-law, Brooks and Dean Phillips, and their kids, Sydney and Trey. Kyle and I live on the other part of the ranch. We calve out about 700 cows, running Simmental cross cattle and a small bunch of full-blooded Fleckvieh Simmentals—which are the source of some of our home-raised breeding bulls. We put up all our own hay for the cattle to eat during winter.

Kyle is president of the volunteer fire

department, and I teach high school math and junior high math and English in Drummond, a town about 20 miles away. I also started 3G Beef (a business entity separate from the ranch). The cattle market can be tough, and price fluctuations make it hard to rely on a consistent income. By marketing directly to consumers, 3G is able to get a more consistent price for our product.

On my days off, you'll often find me outside with our kids helping Kyle on the ranch. In early June we prepare cattle for breeding season. This means making sure the grass in the pastures has grown enough and fences are strong, turning water onto our fields to grow winter hay forage, and ensuring the cows and calves are vaccinated and branded and the bulls are ready to be turned out.

We devote the first week of June to turning out bulls and artificially inseminating (AI-ing) heifers so we can keep their due dates grouped together in mid-March. This makes them easier to monitor. We used to aim for late February, but we made the change because of 2018's winter storms that dropped tons of snow and brought temperatures between 40 and 50 degrees below zero.

A BEEFY BALANCING ACT

June 1 You may have seen a circus act involving a juggler balancing on an unstable platform. This is the best metaphor I can come up with for being in Montana's cattle industry during May and June.

Because I just finished teaching for the year, I can help facilitate AI-ing and turning out bulls. Natalie and Reid are still in school, so they do their chores before getting on the bus. Kadin graduated from eighth grade last Thursday, so we have his help all week. Natalie and Kadin typically take turns feeding the 4-H animals, and Reid tags along. Today Natalie fed Mo and Larry

After a long day of ranch work, Tressa prepares 3G beef for dinner.

(the 4-H steers) and Drake (a bull calf from Kadin's 4-H beef breeding project).

Our nephew, Trey, met us at the corrals south of Browns Lake (about an 8-mile drive from home) to help prep for AI-ing. Jose Rodriguez and Miguel Acosta, seasonal workers hired through the H-2A program, were there, too. We put up an electric fence so the cows can access water while pastured near the corrals.

Trey is also working on a conifer encroachment project with Natural Resources Conservation Service and their Targeted Implementation Plan (TIP) program. Encroaching conifer trees choke out grasses that support native elk, deer and bird populations. The project works to conserve native grasses and maintain soil health.

Natalie feeds grain to the 4-H cows. She and her big brother, Kadin, take turns with this task, and Reid often tags along.

June 2 Yesterday was long, but it ended with watching the kids play baseball. Today will be long, too, but I don't mind being outside on these gorgeous days, caring for animals and enjoying the beauty of our land.

Kadin went to the lake corrals to help heat-detect cows that may be ready to AI this evening. Kyle drove to Bozeman to get equipment for haying season, tires for our irrigation pivots and a repaired irrigation pump motor for the pivots across the river. Later Kadin, Jose and Miguel filled water tanks for the AI cows, fixed fences and took gravel to fix a boggy alleyway in the corrals.

June 3 We met Travis Cline from Cline Genetics at the lake corrals for AI-ing. Kadin and Kyle brought in heifers and pairs to sort. All of the AI-ed heifers got turned out for the start of their summer rotation, and cleanup bulls were ready to breed any heifers that didn't take the AI.

A storm rolled in with heavy wind, rain and nearby lightning. Luckily it died down before we went back to the lake to finish AI-ing. In the last rays of light, after trailing heifers and filling water and feed, we visited with friends and family who had helped, enjoying the bliss of a good day.

June 4 The heat yesterday was rough, so today we met at 6:30 a.m. After AI-ing, we picked up the water tank and a few cows to haul home. Kyle and Trey checked to see which parts we needed to fix the masticator machine for the conifer project. Kyle loaded up a few bulls for retesting and headed to our veterinarian.

Today was the last day of school for Natalie and Reid. Naw (the kids' nickname for Sue) helped the two older kids practice their speeches for the evening's 4-H demonstration on assisting with calf birthing. After the 4-H meeting, we loaded up Hiram, our bull, and took him to the lake to be the cleanup bull for the AI-ed 4-H and club calf mommas.

June 5 We're behind schedule with branding because Kyle tore out our old corrals, which included some of the original cedar posts that his grandpa had installed. The result? A streamlined, new corral.

Kadin went bear hunting, leaving at about 2 p.m. and getting home after dark. He reminds me of an old mountain man who'd be completely content living off the wilderness in remote backcountry. Kadin hunts and fishes as much as he can. He'll hike miles and miles to get to where he wants to go and not tire. Kyle and I can't keep up with him anymore.

June 6 Each June we try to get away for a vacation, so we have to work double-time to get everything done and scheduled before we leave. Almost without fail, problems arise in the run-up to a getaway. Today a friend brought his boom truck to help set the pump and motor into the river that feeds our upper and lower pivots. We saw there wasn't enough power going to the pivots, so we called the power

Tressa doles out sweet scratches while visiting with some of the kids' 4-H animals.

company to troubleshoot. We mostly resolved the problem, but one pivot is still running incorrectly. An issue for another day.

Meanwhile, we moved Drake to the pasture in front of our house to breed Trey's heifer, Mercedes. Kadin and I recalculated and measured feed rations for Drake, Mercedes and the 4-H steers. Feeding grain is tricky. Dietary changes can cause bloat, so transitioning feeds means consulting with our feed rep to make sure our cattle get the best diet they possibly can.

June 7 When we settle in for the evening, our minds run laps trying to anticipate problems and prioritize the next day's tasks. Eureka! Kyle figured out what was wrong with the pivot in the middle of the night.

Today Kadin and I weighed 4-H steers to monitor their growth and recalculate rations in preparation for the August fair. I weighed 3G beef on a neighbor's scales for the same reason. Kyle made a trip to Missoula to pick up a four-wheeler from the mechanic and get one of our trucks an oil change—a service that comes with a free car wash. With our mud-encrusted ranch vehicles, I imagine the staff play a game of Rock, Paper, Scissors when we roll in, and then the loser has to do the wash.

OLD WOOD AND NATIVE GRASSES

June 8 Kyle and I so appreciate our good water and fertile soil. While traveling through ag lands on our way to the sand dunes, we saw a lot of ranches plagued with drought and dry grasses—sad to see so early in June. We told the kids that if we lived in this part of the state, they'd be doing a lot more rock picking!

June 9 Things were calm back on the ranch, so we had a stress-free, beautiful day together in the dunes. At the end of the day, Kyle dealt with pivot issues on the phone with Jose. Great news! They got it running.

June 11 Home! Kyle took care of some minor pivot issues, and the kids and I checked on 4-H animals and 3G beef. Natalie took Mo a treat, which he munched on while she scratched him in his favorite spots.

June 12 Having an alternative way to heat our house is essential (last winter we were without power for three days), so Kyle and I began redoing our unfinished basement, which includes a wood stove. We are repurposing wood from the old sheep barn Kyle's great-great-grandfather built. Its old floors will become the fireplace mantel—reminding us of our forebears and the long hours they spent caring for their animals.

June 13 We actively monitor our

Kadin, the oldest of the Gravely children, counts cows and watches over the herd.

pastures to give native grasses time to regenerate and reseed. Today Kyle and Kadin moved the cows on Ward Creek to their next grazing spot. You could almost see the moisture being sucked out of the ground as temps crept into the 90s—a worrying sign since summer hasn't officially started.

HAYING, PLAYING AND GRAZING

June 15 We're having problems with the accumulator, a machine attached to the back of the baler that helps bunch bales, so we arranged for our equipment dealer to drop off the parts. I called in instructions to my meat processor, figured future processing dates and brainstormed strategies to promote 3G. I've been advertising on Facebook, but its algorithms now limit the number of people who see posts or ads.

June 16 Last night we watched Kadin play in his first high school basketball scrimmage. Where has the time gone? It seems like yesterday that he was sitting at the family dinner table, dirty from playing with toy tractors—and now he's wearing the dirt and grime of welding real ones.

June 17 Last year we put in several raised beds using old water tanks and culverts to make it easier to prep the soil without a rototiller. This year I'm planning to grow peas, lettuce, beans and carrots. I used a tractor to get compost for the beds.

During lunch, Kyle watched an online cattle sale to figure out when to contract our calves. Several lots went 20 cents back; it's disheartening to see ranchers taking a hit on their heifers. In the afternoon we prepped haying equipment—changing oil, greasing machines and checking tire pressures—and we replaced the cutting knives on the swather. Our yard looked like a dealership!

June 19 Yesterday Kyle ran to town to get supplies for the coming months. Once haying starts, trips to town will become nonexistent. Today some two- and three-year-old mommas and late calving pairs had to be moved to their next field. Some background: In our lower pivot, Kyle built an intensive grazing rotation with nine different cells. Eight are irrigated by the pivot. This improves soil health, in turn helping grass regenerate and providing native bird species with undisturbed nesting habitat. With this rotation in play, we're able to expand our herd while decreasing the expense of haying and farming this particular pivot.

June 20 Weather can make or break a ranch, so we appreciate the 4.5 inches of rain we've received since the start of May.

Much of our state thirsts for precipitation. We celebrated Father's Day with a family brunch at our local restaurant.

June 21 Out the door running! I helped the kids halter and practice leading their 4-H steers. We think Natalie's gentle giant, Mo, will finish at a little more than 1,300 pounds. An 80-pound kid handling a steer that size will be something to see!

Later we dealt with a blown hose on a tractor and fixed the masticator so Trey can continue the TIP project. Kyle leveled the fill material on a road project on the west side of the lake.

We enjoyed the remnants of the day fishing and kayaking on Browns Lake. We try to squeeze in these activities on long, busy days.

MACHINERY WOES AND LAUNDRY

June 22 In ranching, many of the same things happen day after day. But there's always a surprise or two that sneak up to remind us we aren't on cruise control. When the kids ask Kyle, "What are we doing tomorrow?" his response is always, "I don't know. Wait until tomorrow."

Lately our surprises have been early morning phone calls letting us know our cows are on the highway. Sometimes it's a broken fence or gates that have been left open by trespassers. We're thankful for our neighbors, who help keep the cows safe by making those calls.

June 23 Machinery prices have skyrocketed over the last decade while calf prices have remained the same or dropped. So, we fix stuff—suck it up and grab a wrench.

Yesterday the tractor we use for everything, from hauling gravel to stacking hay, blew two high-pressure hydraulic hoses. The hoses are way up underneath the cab, so banged-up knuckles are guaranteed when you're the one doing the fixing.

June 24 After morning chores, Kyle ordered parts for ATVs, dirt bikes and haying equipment. Trey went back to welding on the bucket of the old Versatile, and Jose and Miguel drove out to the lake to cut conifers for the TIP project.

June 25 The kids haltered and walked their steers, then tied them up and practiced running water over them. The animals were so quiet, no doubt because of the time Kadin and Natalie spend graining them, talking to them and loving on them.

June 26 Mealtimes can get wild because of the long daylight hours. Sometimes breakfast is a granola bar and lunch happens after a surprised glance at the clock shows it's already 2 p.m. Dinner may not happen until the sun sets near 10 p.m. Natalie is a big help—often she makes sandwiches or pasta to feed the troops. I'm so proud when our kids step up!

June 27 The worst items of clothing to take care of are calving coveralls—the ones that stand up by themselves. You can't simply throw them into the machine. You have to hang them on the fence and pressure-wash them first. When guests visit on laundry day, they look concerned when they hear my washing machine on its last cycle. I smile and gesture to the laundry room. "I'm taking my jet to the Bahamas. Want to come?"

June 28 Kyle and I are taking the kids on our annual family river float before we get into haying. We'll float all day tomorrow and come home on Wednesday.

June 29 Haying started today while we were rafting. The alfalfa was ready, and the forecast said hot and dry for the next 15 days. If the hay doesn't get cut when it's ready, its nutritional value decreases.

June 30 Pivot five was knocked down today. Hay is drying fast in the heat, so we can't take any more down until we get the balers going. We will start raking early tomorrow morning, as the dew helps keep the leaves soft and prevents them from crumbling in the heat. Crumbled leaves offer less protein—a nutrient essential for animals that endure the unforgiving cold of our winters. One of our most important jobs is to make sure the cows are healthy and happy.

I love June—its long workdays sprinkled with fun family time, the lush green emerging from its winter dormancy and cows lounging in our wide-open spaces. But where did the month go? It seems just last week we were kicking out pairs, AI-ing and turning out bulls. Time marches on no matter how hard we try to anchor ourselves in the moment. What we do may not always be easy, but we are grounded, and I am thankful.

YOU SAY TOMATO

In Virginia, a father and son re-imagined their century farm.
Now, they're helping it grow.

HERBERT BROWN JR. WITH HERBERT BROWN SR. WARFIELD, VA

My dad, Herbert Brown Sr., and I are small farmers in Southside Virginia—an area that stretches from the James River south to the North Carolina border. Together we own and operate Browntown Farms, where we raise strawberries, blueberries, grape tomatoes and other seasonal produce.

Our farm was founded in 1908 and has been officially recognized as a century farm. It originally included 348 acres of land, which my great-great-grandfather Sandy Brown and his brother-in-law Collins Jackson purchased for $1,200. Over the years the land was split among various family members, and my dad and

I now have 114 acres of woodland and cropland acreage.

Today we are produce farmers, but that wasn't always the case. Historically, our roots are tied to raising tobacco as a cash crop. Almost two decades after our family got out of the tobacco business, my dad and I decided to rehabilitate the farm to grow vegetables. This transition involved clearing trees from overgrown fields and amending the soil to make it suitable for crop production. We chose to get into vegetables because it was the least expensive option to transition to. We couldn't afford to get back into tobacco because of the expense of equipment and labor and the lack of modern-day tobacco-handling infrastructure.

The establishment period wasn't easy, and we still feel that every day is a learning experience. Although our farm is more than 100 years old, we're still putting the puzzle pieces together. The journey never stops! It has taken us more than 15 years of consistent investment to accumulate the right plants, infrastructure and equipment, and while we have come a long way, we still have a way to go to fulfill our vision for the farm.

Agriculture is a lifestyle, and you have to love it to stay in the game. You have to embrace the wins and accept the losses. Every day we wake up with a purpose, and it feels good to have meaning behind our work.

We love building relationships, and we take pride in what we do because others appreciate us and find value in what we do. Here at Browntown Farms, we extend the "Know your farmer, know your food" concept to every customer. We want everyone to leave the farm feeling as if they are a part of the Browntown family. We all have call lists of specific people upon whom we depend: people with professions like doctor, barber, mechanic and lawyer. Ultimately, everyone should have a farmer or two on that list.

One of our farm's most significant aims is to add value to everything from our crops to people's everyday lives. Black farmers make up less than 2% of the farming population, so being a Black farmer is valuable in and of itself, in that we represent an important facet of

Herbert Jr. (left) and his dad, Herbert Sr., grade and pack their grape tomatoes for sale—only fully ripe and blemish free tomatoes make it into the containers.

We want everyone to leave the farm feeling as if they are part of the family.

the country's farming history and we demonstrate for others that it can be done. We are proud to carry on my family's farming heritage and add value to our product in the process.

One way we do this is by creating small-batch gourmet jams. Our slogan is "We make farm-fresh taste so jam delicious." Each time we put our farm in a jar, it gives our highly perishable berries a longer shelf life and allows folks outside of the region to enjoy the products of our farm. Finding our niche in this market has been great, because it gives us a shippable product that allows us to reach people across the entire United States. It also helps boost our cash flow during the winter months.

We also strive to improve access to fresh

Named for legendary boxer Joe Lewis (the Brown Bomber), the Browns' farm dog goes by "Bummer." He protects the fields and loves the camera.

food in our area. We all know eating healthy helps prevent medical issues and may reduce doctor's visits. Alongside various partners, our goal is to create a distribution model that brings good food within reach of everyone. Combating food deserts is a priority here since our county has only one grocery store.

We will soon add value to our farm through agricultural tourism. There is a huge disconnect between the general population and ag, and as a result, there is a need to educate people about farm life and the origin of the food they eat every day. Our goal is to increase awareness among youth and adults by hosting farm tours, events and activities. Tourism and agriculture are among Virginia's top industries, so we see a future in becoming a destination farm.

POTTING & PLANTING COLLARDS

July 1 Today was hot—and, unfortunately, we experienced compressor issues with the freezer where we'd intended to store our recently harvested berries. These berries will be used to make our Browntown jams.

On the plus side, we finalized the jar label order for our blackberry lemonade and blueberry lemonade jams. The two new flavors will join our current jam assortment: strawberry, triple berry, strawberry habanero, strawberry peach and strawberry lemonade. Our jams are made at Prince Edward Cannery in Farmville, Virginia, and this batch will be ready for sale by the end of July.

July 2 Yesterday's much-needed rain cooled things off, which is great news for the crops! (We enjoyed the more pleasant temperatures today, too.) The sky was partly cloudy and rainy, making it a perfect day for picking cucumbers in a hoop house. We also picked kale, blackberries and onions. Tomorrow we'll pick one of our later rabbiteye varieties of blueberries.

July 3 Many of our customers are preparing to celebrate the Fourth of July with family and friends—and so are we! Later in the day we joined our friends at Seven Springs Farm and Vineyard in Norlina, North Carolina, to enjoy live music and magnificent wine.

July 4 Today was a good day. We began it with breakfast outside in our farm park area. It was nice to catch up with family and friends and enjoy the holiday. After gathering eggs and feeding the chickens, we took a slight break from the farm, heading back to Seven Springs in the evening to introduce our family to this amazing venue.

July 5 My dad and I picked cucumbers and blackberries, then planted Morris Heading, Vates, and Champion collard greens before harvesting squash.

Next, we graded grape tomatoes and packaged them for an upcoming sale. When grading, we identify the tomatoes that are fully ripe and free of blemishes. Those that have splits or don't meet our size standards will not make their way into the clamshell containers for sale.

As we do every day, we also fed the chickens and gave them fresh water.

July 6 The grape tomatoes are getting ripe fast, so we spent a few hours harvesting them. As the sun shines brighter, the temperatures increase in our hoop houses (they can reach more than 100 degrees), so we try to finish our daily harvest before midday.

Because of the heat, we hurried to do a quick 15-minute picking of eggplants and cucumbers in a separate high tunnel. For the rest of the workday we met with customers at the farm stand and filled recent orders.

July 7 Today we continued to prepare for our fall collard crop. To start, we potted 1,000 collard seeds in trays; it will take 4 to 6 weeks for them to be ready for transplanting into the ground.

Next, we picked cucumbers and string beans—the latter is a customer favorite. To further prepare for fall, we used our push planter to plant six 150-foot-long rows of collard green seeds. Growth from this seedbed will be planted next month along with the other collards for fall harvest. After that, we irrigated crops in two of our high tunnels and hopped on the lawn mower to cut grass around the farm. Around midday, we went to Petersburg to pick up supplies and chicken feed before grading more grape tomatoes.

PICKING, GRADING & PACKAGING TOMATOES

July 8 As we do first thing every morning, we fed the chickens and gave them water. Then we picked cucumbers, peppers and eggplant. After harvesting, we made vegetable boxes that included tomatoes, string beans, potatoes, peppers, zucchini, squash and onions. Next, we graded and packaged grape tomatoes.

July 9 More picking today! We harvested squash and cucumbers in the morning. Before midday we also harvested tomatoes and made more mixed vegetable boxes for customers to pick up during the evening hours. We gathered eggs and fed chickens before calling it a day.

July 10 Southside Virginia was beautiful today; the sun was bright and the birds were chirping. In the morning, we fulfilled an order of fresh vegetables for Nomad Deli in Richmond. Our cousins run this wonderful restaurant, and if you are in the area with a huge appetite, you have to try the Hog Rider: a 12-inch sub featuring a pound of meat on rye. (Tell 'em Browntown sent ya!)

We ended the day by packaging grape tomatoes and gathering eggs.

July 11 We got an early start picking grape tomatoes before the sun got too hot. After harvesting, we graded more tomatoes and placed them in clamshell containers. Any that we find damaged or too small get fed to our chickens.

We ran irrigation in the hoop houses today. Hot days can affect the plants, so we have to monitor water supply and soil moisture. As the day cooled down, it was grass-cutting time until dark.

July 12 Today we picked more tomatoes and graded our harvest. We then placed excess clamshells in storage, wiped the table down and swept the floor of the market area to prepare for customers. Just like yesterday, today ended with cutting grass and gathering eggs before dark.

Left: Herbert Sr. hands fresh-picked sweet bell peppers to his son for a produce-box customer. Right: Perhaps best known for its strawberries and small-batch jams, Browntown Farms also grows squash, collard greens, cucumbers, eggplant and tomatoes, as well as other seasonal fruits and veggies.

Herbert Jr. moves mushroom compost to prepare ground for planting.

July 13 Where there is land, there is grass to cut. Today we cut grass—again! We also tied some of our tomato plants with twine to keep them growing upright. This step helps the plants stay off the ground, which keeps the tomatoes clean and helps prevent disease. Then we ran irrigation to saturate the soil before planting peppers in the high tunnel.

July 14 Today started with the usual task of feeding the chickens and giving them water. And did I mention that there's always grass to cut? After getting off the lawn mower, we replaced the water pump on our 1976 John Deere 2640 tractor. Next, it was time to Bush Hog the area around the pond.

PREPARING FOR AUTUMN

July 15 Big harvest day: We picked cucumbers, blackberries, peppers and tomatoes. When it rains, it pours! Today the tractor's radiator went out, and we ordered parts over the phone.

Next, we cultivated sweet potatoes by loosening soil on the row beds and row middles. This prevents grass from growing and helps the water penetrate — the soil. After that, we gathered vegetables and prepared customer orders.

July 17 Tomatoes, tomatoes and more tomatoes! That's July for you. Today we harvested, graded and packaged more grape tomatoes.

July 18 We graded tomatoes, then packaged them for a wholesale order. We sell wholesale to small grocery stores, CSA businesses and other distributors—about 75% of our grape tomato business is done in the wholesale market. We picked blueberries during the evening after the temperatures cooled down.

July 19 We continued getting ready for fall by planting 600 young Georgia collard greens in trays. We plant multiple varieties of collard greens because different types have different growing characteristics. Some plants grow upright; this means the leaves stay clean, which is helpful when bunching leaves for traditional wholesale orders. Other varieties produce larger heads, which some retail customers prefer to individual bunches of greens. Later we removed grass and weeds from the high tunnels. We also planted more peppers that we will harvest later in the season.

July 20 More grape tomatoes! Harvest, grading and packing. As you can tell, tomatoes keep us really busy during the summer months. Although it is a labor-intensive crop, customers love them and tell us that our local tomatoes taste better than other ones in the store.

July 21 Today we Bush Hogged the fields and cut grass around the house, then we graded and delivered nine cases of grape tomatoes to the Richmond area. On the way home, we made a pit stop to purchase trash bags and cleaning supplies for the farm. We ended the day by picking cucumbers and gathering eggs.

MEETING WITH CUSTOMERS

July 22 Tractor parts arrived today, and we installed a new radiator. Thankfully now the old Deere is back up and running.

July 23 Today was a vegetable-picking day. We met with customers and assembled produce boxes per their requests. We love meeting the people who love our products! And we especially love when they share the recipe ideas that they use to cook our fresh vegetables.

July 24 The hoop houses are in need of maintenance. To avoid the heat, we cleaned a bit in the early morning and again in the evening. It's important to stay on top of grass and weeds. If left unchecked, they can become competition for the marketable crops.

July 25 The word for today is tomatoes, and picking is the name of the game. Ripe and ready, the crop started to produce heavily this week. Today we picked more than 100 pounds of grape tomatoes!

July 26 Can you guess what today's focus was? That's right: grape tomatoes (again). Picking, grading and packaging.

July 27 We sorted and bagged red potatoes to get them ready for sales over the next week. We also packaged 21 cases of tomatoes, then fed and watered up the chickens.

July 28 Today we cleaned out our cold storage unit where we keep the fresh produce cool. Cold storage extends shelf life and ensures that customers are getting the freshest quality produce. After cleaning it out, we picked squash, cucumbers and zucchini, then packaged more cases of grape tomatoes.

July 29 This morning we fed the chickens and gave them fresh water. We graded more grape tomatoes and irrigated our high tunnel crops. After irrigating, we pulled weeds and watered our collard green seed beds. These will be transplanted in August and harvested in the fall.

July 30 Virginia State University reopened its 416-acre Randolph Farm for an Agriculture Field Day today. (The research farm, which is located in Petersburg, had been closed to the public since the COVID pandemic began.) We attended, of course! These types of educational field days have been critical to the success of our operation. Not only do we learn from knowledgeable extension agents, but we also get the chance to learn from and talk with other farmers as well. Here's a shoutout to VSU for helping small farmers throughout the state!

July 31 Today we had a chance to catch up with a few longtime customers. We enjoy being folks' farmers, and we find joy in building relationships and providing fresh produce to households that love great-tasting food.

It's been a busy, hot month. Harvest is in full swing and fall is coming. We will soon transition from summer to fall produce, and the work will continue. We always get excited about the fall season because the weather is cooler, there are fewer problematic insects and the grass starts to slow down in the fields. Also, fall signals the start of the peak selling season for our strawberry jam. Before you know it, we'll be shipping out jams for Christmas!

The two Herberts are the fourth and fifth generations at Browntown, a tobacco farm turned produce operation.

Scrapbook

CAPTURE THE BEAUTY AROUND YOU

2

1. CATCH THE SUN

I planted sunflowers all over the yard in hopes of attracting more birds. One morning a pair of goldfinches were eagerly checking out the sunflowers to see if the seeds were ready to eat. The seeds weren't quite ripe yet, but I captured this photo of the male goldfinch.

ANDY RAUPP MONTELLO, WI

2. EVENING STROLL

What a joy to see our son, Brady, enjoying a beautiful summer evening on the farm.

JAMI MOFFATT NEW CASTLE, PA

1. BUBBLES & BOOTS
Our sons are named for towns in Texas in tribute to their father, Austin. Here, Tyler takes full advantage of the nice summer weather for an outdoor soak.

BRANDI ANDERSON WEST PLAINS, MO

2. PRETTY MAIDS ALL IN A ROW
Cats are naturally curious. Kittens are probably even more so, as they are just beginning to explore and learn about the world around them.

ELIZABETH EVERSOLE OLEOSSIAN, IA

3. BEST BUDS
Josh, my son, was hanging out in the feed bunk of our family farm when a curious heifer sneaked up behind him to say hello.

ANGIE CROW ARNOLD, NE

1. LEARNING TO STEER
Here is a photo of our sons, Lyle and Koen, riding their pedal tractor after my husband repainted it for them.

ERIKA KIMM MANHATTAN, MT

2. MORNING MEETING
While on an early morning summer walk in Bells Bend Park in Nashville, Tennessee, I observed some incredible bird activity. A male blue grosbeak with an insect let out repeated metallic calls, alarming his neighbors. An orchard oriole pair came to investigate. Just as the three birds landed on the same stalk, I captured this image. Being able to witness this feather frenzy was truly a magical moment.

MARY GLYNN WILLIAMSON NASHVILLE, TN

3. GENTLE GIANT
Gunner the Great Pyrenees likes watching over our farm. My husband and I have both lost family members, and Gunner has helped us through so many tough times.

TAMMY BEACHLEY MIDDLETOWN, MD

BATH TIME

One a warm day a few years ago, we put our birdbath outside. Almost immediately this Anna's hummingbird began splashing around in it. It went from pool to pool on the waterfall and seemed to enjoy washing its beak.

REG ROBAZZA SURREY, BC

1. BERRY CUTE

My daughter Ellis, 2, is full of life—and love for everyone she meets. She especially enjoys spending time with her horse, Sugar, and feeding her fresh berries when they're in season!

ANGELINA SPREWELL SWEETWATER, TN

2. SPRAYING IT COOL

On hot days, Kale and his Pappy like riding through the sprinklers. They sometimes set up small obstacle courses or make mud pits to drive through. Whatever they choose, they are making memories to last a lifetime.

JOYCE WILSON LEWISTOWN, PA

3. GREETINGS, FARM FRIEND!

Our granddaughter, Myla, enjoys spending time on our farm. She doesn't care if she's in a fancy dress or her play clothes. Farm life is for her!

KEN MILLER SOUTH VIENNA, OH

1. KITTY-UP, COWBOY

Felix was a part of our ranch for several years. More like a dog than a cat, he was house-trained (no litter box, he'd simply let himself outside) and he "helped" with everything. You could talk to him and he would talk right back! A special cat, for sure.

AMBER ANDERSON COTTONWOOD, ID

2. OUT OF THE BLUE

It's a pleasure to photograph spectacular indigo buntings every summer. I snapped this photo at home when the bunting found a spot among the wildflowers.

RONALD GREENE CHESTERLAND, OH

3. LEARNING ON THE JOB

Zachary, 7, is a sixth-generation farmer learning the family trade. He is following in his elders' footsteps, and he is always there to help out—whether raking hay or giving his dad or grandpa a ride in the Gator.

HOPE SMITH SHELOCTA, PA

3

1. CENTURY-FARM FROLICS
Parker explores the Oklahoma wheat field that has been farmed by our family for six generations. Behind him you can see his great-great grandfather's barn.

COURTNEY HARGIS-MCCLURE ALLEN, TX

2. MEET AND GREET
Our granddaughter Reese was so excited to meet Blondie. It was love at first sight for both of them!

CHRYSTAL HUENEKE MAQUOKETA, IA

3. SPEEDY DELIVERY
I liked raising chickens as a child, and my husband and I thought it'd be fun for our kids. The day after we brought our hens home, my son got up at 6 a.m. to check for eggs—and he found one!

ALESHA ERDENBERGER GLEN HAVEN, WI

1. DIVE IN

I consider myself a true bluebird landlord after five years of hosting a mated pair of bluebirds. They stay in the backyard year-round and raise three broods every year. I like to feed them live mealworms from decorative bowls that I usually find at thrift shops. When I took this picture, my first thought was that it resembles me when I'm given a bowl of ice cream!

REBECCA BOYD KNOXVILLE, TN

2. PRIORITIES IN ORDER

My father-in-law, Frank, was mowing hay by our house. He loves his grandkids, and as soon as he saw us coming toward him, he stopped the tractor to talk to little Lila.

MELANIE HARVEY ELLISTON, VA

3. SHE'S NO QUACK!

Our Jorja loves visiting Grandma Judy's farm, with all its ducks, chickens and pigs. She loves all animals and says she wants to be a veterinarian when she grows up.

JILL PERKEREWICZ EAST GRAND FORKS, MN

Heart & Soul

WORDS TO LIVE BY

Linguist Lynette St. Clair uses modern technology to preserve
the language of her ancestors

ASHLEY ABRAMSON WIND RIVER INDIAN RESERVATION, WY

Around 40 years ago, Lynette St. Clair saw a documentary about a woman in Washington state who was the last native language speaker left in her tribe. "When they asked her how to say *fish*, a word that is so prominent in the Pacific Northwest, she couldn't remember," Lynette recalls. "I didn't want to be that person, so I made a promise to myself and to my grandparents that I'd never forget my own language."

A lifelong resident of the Wind River Indian Reservation in Wyoming, Lynette grew up hearing and speaking Shoshone. Her parents were fluent speakers, and she frequently spent time around her extended family, all of whom spoke the language together. Now she's a linguist who is dedicated to preserving the Shoshone language for future generations, partly through a new app she has developed for use in schools.

GIVING BACK

Language is more than just a means of communication. Lynette describes it, first and foremost, as a way to connect spiritually with a person's ancestors and land. "Our language is descriptive," she says, "and it's our responsibility to know and understand the sacred places and spaces our grandparents named."

She also believes in sharing her culture with those who ask about it. "I was always told that when people ask you for help, you answer that call," Lynette says. With that idea in mind, she accepted a job at Fort Washakie Schools, the same school system

Lynette St. Clair has been a lifelong resident of the Wind River Indian Reservation in Wyoming.

that she attended, to help carry Shoshone culture to the next generation.

After working in the office there for several years, Lynette took on a new role as Indian education coordinator in 2007. From the outset, she was surprised by how little her students knew of their culture, including their language. "The language is not as vibrant in our community today as it was when I was growing up," she says.

Her first big initiative was developing a holistic education program focused on teaching K-12 students about the tribe's history, culture and language. During the month of January, for example, Shoshone people traditionally move from home to home, telling stories in honor of that month's moon phase. As Lynette teaches

> *I made a promise to myself and to my grandparents that I'd never forget my own language.*

Lynette created the Shoshone Language App to provide virtual instruction to people interested in learning her tribe's language.

technology more fully. A few years ago, one of her friends sent her a recording from the 1930s of an American general meeting with Shoshone tribal leaders.

In the clip, the general and leaders communicated using North American Indian Sign Language, which was once the universal language of many indigenous tribes. Immediately, Lynette recognized a familiar face on the screen: her great-great-grandfather Dick Washakie. The experience cemented both the promise she made to carry their language forward and the means by which she was doing it.

"It was mind-blowing to see him using the technology of the time to document his language," she says. "It was a sign that I needed to continue teaching with technology so that in a hundred years people might be able to learn from it."

FINDING A PATH FORWARD

So far Lynette has worked on two apps. The first, called Shoshone Language App, provides virtual instruction for anyone who wants to learn the language. Because Shoshone is exclusively a spoken language, Lynette is also working to develop an orthography—or writing system—which will be taught in the app. With help from her older students, Lynette also developed a virtual tour for an app called TravelStorysGPS, offering photo and audio tours of the Shoshone portion of the Wind River Indian Reservation. (The land is also home to the Arapaho tribe.)

While Lynette sees her work as a way to promote Shoshone culture within her tribe, she is also hopeful that non-Indigenous Americans will learn about their native neighbors and perhaps use the knowledge they gain to overcome harmful stereotypes.

"People look at us as relics of the past, but we're living, breathing human beings," she explains. "We are businesspeople, lawyers, judges and educators. We are still here. See us."

her students about the value of family, she incorporates relevant language lessons into her coursework.

LEARNING THE LANGUAGE

Shoshone, Lynette admits, is complex and can be hard to learn, but its difficulty hasn't deterred her students' excitement. They often ask her how to say words and phrases they don't know, and kids who grasp the lessons more quickly often help others overcome learning challenges.

"I try to have them leave English at the door when they come into the classroom, and it's been encouraging to see them actually do that," she says. Technology and social media have made engaging with the language easier for her students, and recently Lynette developed a new tool to help teach Shoshone culture both inside and outside the classroom.

Lynette has always been comfortable incorporating technology into her lesson plans, but she recalls a specific lightbulb moment that encouraged her to embrace

FRESHLY PICKED

There's nothing sweeter than a summer day spent
gathering raspberries with a loved one

KAREN GIEBEL REPUBLIC, WA

Have you ever experienced a sudden flood of memories out of the blue? That happened to me once while walking along a dirt road near my house. I spotted some plump blackberries growing wild by a fence.

When I saw them, I was struck by a memory of my dad and the summers I spent picking black raspberries with him on our family farm.

Black raspberries ripen in July in New York state. Dad expected me to spend part of my summer vacation picking them. Any farmer will tell you that they need to be picked before the sun starts to dry them out, and I did not love being hustled out of bed so early. But I loved the sweetness of those shiny black gems. And I loved knowing that when I returned after a morning spent searching for berries, my mom would be waiting for me in the kitchen, ready to make batch after batch of jam. To this day, her jam is still my favorite fruit spread. I'd slather it, fresh from the stove, on homemade bread. No snack was better.

For lunch she'd serve us bowls of black raspberries drenched in canned milk and sugar. And when we brought her more berries than she could use right away, she'd freeze the extras in quart containers so that they'd be ready for winter pies.

At some point each summer, friends would wander over to our house and the raspberry wars would begin. We'd throw berries across the tops of the bushes, trying to stain each other purple.

Today, black raspberries are hard to find in grocery stores and cost their weight in gold. Back then, Dad spread them out on a table by the road and sold them for 45 cents a quart. Times have changed!

When I was a kid, I didn't like getting up early to pick those berries. But on that day, as I stood in front of the patch of berries by the side of the road, I found myself wishing my dad was standing there with me, urging me to get up and pick berries with him.

Karen Giebel grew up on a farm in New York, where her parents grew their own vegetables and berries.

LEVEL GROUND

A dairy farming father's love for his family
lives on in the tools that he left behind

CHERYL SPECK EDGERTON, KS

I nside a junk drawer, surrounded by packs of chewing gum and a motley collection of discarded hardware pieces, I found the tool I was looking for.

It was my dad's old level—neon green and 9 inches long. "Made in the USA. The Boss 591-9" was printed near its center.

Levels and plumb lines offer up proof of accuracy—evidence of a rational and well-ordered world.

Both will probably always remind me of my father, Clayton Stoker.

My dad owned a dairy farm for 40 years. He led his Holsteins into their barn stalls twice each day, 365 days a year, to milk them. At 4 a.m. every day, he was up and ready to start working, regardless of the weather. He rarely took vacations. And when he was forced to sell his herd, he still managed to pay the bills for a while longer by harvesting corn and soybeans.

That all changed in 1984, the year that the nation's farm crisis peaked. Dad lost everything: his land, home and livestock. The loss stung, but he managed to find his equilibrium again.

He became a carpenter. Each morning he would get dressed and put on a worn leather tool belt. Inside the belt's pockets he kept a tape measure, a spiral notebook, a box knife and—of course—his level.

In 2014, after 60 years on their farm, my parents came to live with me. I took so many photographs: pictures of them cradling their youngest great-grandbabies in their arms and posing proudly alongside their older grandchildren.

Levels and plumb lines offer up proof of accuracy— evidence of a rational and well-ordered world.

Mom had dementia, and it led to sudden outbursts of verbal abuse. Though it was clear that her words hurt him, Dad never once raised his voice or lost his temper. He could have taught a master class in unconditional love.

Eventually, Mom succumbed to pneumonia. But even while grieving, Dad maintained his routine. Walking, tending his tomato patch and reading the *Kansas City Star* cover to cover.

In 2020, just weeks before the COVID-19 lockdowns began, he moved into a long-term care facility. Our window visits tested his patience. I feared they'd crush his spirit, too, but I was wrong. My father stayed strong.

Dad eluded the virus for eight months, but then he caught it. His seven-day battle with COVID ended last November.

Afterward, I was emotionally adrift. Anger and sadness precluded healing. But Dad's example ultimately led me to action. He was the model, and he left me all the tools I needed.

Cheryl Speck poses here with her late father, Clayton Stoker: a veteran, farmer and all-around great dad.

PIANO RECITAL

The sound of her mother's music carried through the air and across the years

MARY JUDITH FINA CHARDON, OH

One of the few places in this world where peace and quiet still make an occasional appearance is in the country on summer mornings.

As a 9-year-old girl living in Newbury, Ohio, in 1957, I used to let the sights and sounds of the natural world wake me up each morning. When the sun started shining into my room, slanting across my face, I would slowly open my eyes. After a few minutes spent listening to the birds chirping and the bees buzzing outside my window, I was usually ready to get up and greet the day.

Only maybe a dozen cars and perhaps one or two trucks passed by our house all day. As such, our home was usually quiet, except for that distant hum of birds and bees. It was an idyllic setting for my mom to sit at our piano and fill the house with the loveliest music I ever experienced.

My mother taught piano lessons, and when my parents bought their first house, they hauled her piano over from my grandparents' house to our new home, where it was given a prominent place.

Mom had a special fondness for classical music, and I eventually inherited a small stack of classical music books from her. I have a book of waltzes (my dad loved waltzes), the "William Tell Overture" by Gioachino Rossini, and *Robbins Mammoth Collection of Famous Piano Music*. Every once in a while Mom got a little funky and played some modern music by jazz pianist Eddy Duchin too.

My father enjoyed a lively polka and even the occasional Hank Williams song. But, for the most part, both of my parents preferred classical music. My dad actually asked my mother out on their first date while they stood in line for opera tickets. Once married with kids, they worked hard to instill a love of opera in their children—though they realized their oldest daughter was a lost cause once the British invaded.

Even during the height of Beatlemania, I still appreciated my mom's piano recitals. It took my dad a little more than an hour to commute home from work. My mom would prepare supper in the afternoon, then sit down at the piano around 4:30 p.m. and play until he came through the door. He insisted that he could hear her playing a quarter of a mile away.

Sometimes, on especially warm, quiet summer days, I imagine that I can still hear her, too.

Mary Judith Fina's parents, Nick and Mary Rose, bonded over their shared love of music.

Taste of the Country

GREEN BEAN, CORN & BUTTERMILK SALAD

PREP 25 min. **COOK** 15 min. + chilling
MAKES 6 servings

- ½ cup reduced-fat mayonnaise
- ½ cup buttermilk
- ½ cup shredded Parmesan cheese, plus more for topping
- 1 Tbsp. lemon juice
- 1 tsp. Worcestershire sauce
- ½ tsp. garlic powder
- ½ tsp. salt
- ½ tsp. pepper
- ¾ lb. fresh green beans, trimmed and cut into 1-in. pieces
- 4 medium ears sweet corn
- 1 Tbsp. olive oil

1. In a small bowl, whisk mayonnaise, buttermilk, ½ cup Parmesan, lemon juice, Worcestershire sauce and seasonings. Refrigerate, covered, until serving.
2. Meanwhile, in a Dutch oven, bring 8 cups water to a boil. Add beans; cook, uncovered, just until crisp-tender, 2-3 minutes. Drain and immediately drop into ice water. Drain again and pat dry; transfer to a serving bowl.
3. Cut corn kernels from cobs. In a large heavy skillet, heat oil over medium-high heat. Add corn; cook until tender, 6-8 minutes. Remove from heat; add to beans; refrigerate, covered, until chilled.
4. Add mayonnaise mixture to vegetables; toss to coat. Sprinkle with additional Parmesan.

1 CUP 201 cal., 12g fat (3g sat. fat), 13mg chol., 498mg sod., 20g carb. (8g sugars, 3g fiber), 7g pro.

CORN DOGS

TAKES 25 min. **MAKES** 10 servings

- ¾ cup yellow cornmeal
- ¾ cup self-rising flour
- 1 large egg, lightly beaten
- ⅔ cup 2% milk
- 10 skewers or pop sticks
- 10 hot dogs
  Oil for deep-fat frying

1. In a large bowl, combine cornmeal, flour and egg. Stir in milk to make a thick batter; let stand 4 minutes. Insert sticks into hot dogs; dip into batter.
2. In an electric skillet or deep-fat fryer, heat oil to 375°. Fry corn dogs, a few at a time, until golden brown, 6-8 minutes, turning occasionally. Drain on paper towels.

1 CORN DOG 316 cal., 23g fat (7g sat. fat), 45mg chol., 588mg sod., 18g carb. (2g sugars, 1g fiber), 8g pro.

SPICY COWBOY BEANS

PREP 25 min.
COOK: 1½ hours + releasing
MAKES 10 servings

- 4 bacon strips, chopped
- 1 medium onion, chopped
- 2 garlic cloves, minced
- 2 cups reduced-sodium beef broth
- 3 cups water
- 1 pkg. (16 oz.) 16-bean soup mix
- 1 can (10 oz.) diced tomatoes and green chiles, undrained
- 1 can (8 oz.) tomato sauce
- 1 poblano pepper, chopped
- ¼ cup packed brown sugar
- 1 envelope taco seasoning
  Optional: Chopped fresh cilantro, shredded cheddar cheese and sour cream

1. Select saute or browning setting on a 6-qt. electric pressure cooker; adjust for medium heat. Cook bacon until crisp, 4-5 minutes. Add onion and garlic; cook until tender, 5-6 minutes longer. Add beef broth. Cook 30 seconds, stirring to loosen any browned bits from pan. Press cancel.
2. Add the water, bean soup mix, diced tomatoes and green chiles, tomato sauce, poblano pepper, brown sugar and taco seasoning. Lock lid; close pressure-release valve. Adjust to pressure-cook on high for 90 minutes. Then release pressure naturally.
3. If desired, select saute setting and adjust for low heat. Simmer, stirring constantly, until desired consistency. Press cancel. Serve with toppings of your choice.

¾ CUP 245 cal., 6g fat (2g sat. fat), 10mg chol., 1823mg sod., 52g carb. (9g sugars, 21g fiber), 15g pro.

SUMMER BREAKFAST SKILLET

PREP 20 min. **COOK** 15 min.
MAKES 4 servings

½	lb. fresh chorizo or bulk spicy pork sausage
1	medium sweet yellow pepper, chopped
1	medium sweet red pepper, chopped
1	medium onion, chopped
2	small zucchini, chopped
3	medium tomatoes, chopped
2	garlic cloves, minced
1	tsp. paprika
4	large eggs
¼	tsp. salt
¼	tsp. pepper
½	cup shredded cheddar cheese

1. In a large skillet, cook chorizo, peppers and onion over medium heat, until chorizo is cooked, 4-6 minutes, crumbling chorizo; drain. Stir in zucchini, tomatoes, garlic and paprika; cook, covered, until tender, 5-7 minutes.
2. With back of a spoon, make 4 wells in vegetable mixture; break an egg into each well. Sprinkle eggs with salt and pepper. Cook, covered, until egg whites are set and yolks begin to thicken, 4-6 minutes.
3. Remove from heat; sprinkle with cheese. Let stand, covered, until cheese melts, 5 minutes.

1 SERVING 399 cal., 27g fat (10g sat. fat), 250mg chol., 1012mg sod., 13g carb. (6g sugars, 3g fiber), 24g pro.

BERRY SLUSH

PREP 10 min. + freezing **MAKES** 5 qt.

1	pkg. (3 oz.) raspberry or berry blue gelatin
2	cups boiling water
2	cups sugar
1	can (46 oz.) pineapple juice
2	liters ginger ale
4½	cups cold water
1	cup lemon juice
	Optional: Red or blue liquid food coloring; coarse blue sugar; fresh blueberries, raspberries, strawberries and watermelon

1. In a large container, dissolve gelatin in boiling water; stir in sugar until dissolved. Add pineapple juice, ginger ale, cold water and lemon juice. If desired, add red or blue food coloring. Freeze for 8 hours or overnight.
2. Remove from freezer 20 minutes before serving. Stir until mixture is slushy. Meanwhile, moisten rims of chilled glasses with water. If desired, sprinkle sugar on plate; dip rims in sugar. Spoon slushy mixture in glasses. If desired, top with fruit. Serve immediately.

1 CUP 167 cal., 0 fat (0 sat. fat), 0 chol., 18mg sod., 43g carb. (41g sugars, 0 fiber), 1g pro.

SMOKED BRISKET

PREP 20 min. + marinating
COOK 8 hours + standing
MAKES 20 servings

- 2 Tbsp. olive oil
- 1 fresh beef brisket (7 to 8 lbs.), flat cut

RUB

- 2 Tbsp. garlic powder
- 2 Tbsp. onion powder
- 2 Tbsp. chili powder
- 1 Tbsp. ground mustard
- 1 Tbsp. ground cumin
- 1 Tbsp. paprika
- 1 Tbsp. smoked sea salt

MOP SAUCE

- 2 cups beef broth
- ¼ cup olive oil
- 2 Tbsp. Worcestershire sauce
- 2 Tbsp. hickory-flavored liquid smoke

1. Brush olive oil over brisket. Combine rub ingredients; rub over both sides of beef. Place brisket on a rimmed baking sheet. Cover and refrigerate overnight or up to 2 days. Meanwhile, in small saucepan, combine mop sauce ingredients. Simmer 15 minutes, stirring occasionally. Refrigerate until ready to grill.

2. Soak hickory and mesquite chips or pellets; add to smoker according to the manufacturer's directions. Heat to 225°. Uncover brisket. Place in the smoker fat side up; smoke 2 hours. Brush generously with mop sauce; turn meat. Smoke 2 more hours; brush generously with mop sauce again. Wrap brisket securely in heavy-duty aluminum foil; smoke until a thermometer inserted in beef reads 190°, 4-5 more hours.

3. Let beef stand 20-30 minutes before slicing; cut diagonally across the grain into thin slices.

4 OZ. COOKED BEEF 252 cal., 11g fat (3g sat. fat), 68mg chol., 472mg sod., 2g carb. (0 sugars, 1g fiber), 33g pro.

WATERMELON CUPCAKES

PREP 30 min.
BAKE 20 min. + cooling
MAKES 2 dozen

- 1 pkg. white cake mix (regular size)
- 1 cup lemon-lime soda
- 3 large egg whites, room temperature
- ¼ cup canola oil
- 1 pkg. (3 oz.) watermelon gelatin
- 2 drops watermelon oil, optional

FROSTING

- 2 cups butter, softened
- 6 cups confectioners' sugar
- 1 pkg. (3 oz.) watermelon gelatin
- 5 to 6 Tbsp. lemon-lime soda
- 15 drops red food coloring
- 3 Tbsp. miniature semisweet chocolate chips

1. Preheat oven to 350°. Line 24 muffin cups with paper liners. In a large bowl, combine cake mix, lemon-lime soda, egg whites, canola oil, watermelon gelatin and, if desired, watermelon oil. Beat on low speed 30 seconds, then on medium speed 2 minutes. Transfer the batter to the pans. Bake until a toothpick inserted into a cupcake comes out clean, 18-21 minutes. Cool in pans 10 minutes before removing to wire racks to cool completely.

2. For frosting, in a large bowl, combine butter, confectioners' sugar, gelatin, lemon-lime soda and food coloring; beat until smooth. Frost cupcakes, then sprinkle with chocolate chips. Store in the refrigerator.

1 CUPCAKE 385 cal., 19g fat (11g sat. fat), 41mg chol., 282mg sod., 54g carb. (46g sugars, 1g fiber), 2g pro.

HONEY-LIME YOGURT DIP

TAKES 5 min. **MAKES** 2 cups

- 2 cups plain yogurt
- ¼ cup honey
- 2 Tbsp. lime juice
- ½ tsp. grated lime zest
  Assorted fresh fruit

Whisk the yogurt, honey, lime juice and lime zest in a small bowl. Refrigerate until serving. Serve with fruit.

¼ CUP 70 cal., 2g fat (1g sat. fat), 8mg chol., 29mg sod., 12g carb. (12g sugars, 0 fiber), 2g pro.

BLACK RASPBERRY BUBBLE RING

PREP 35 min. + rising **BAKE** 25 min. **MAKES** 1 loaf (16 pieces)

- 1 pkg. (¼ oz.) active dry yeast
- ¼ cup warm water (110° to 115°)
- 1 cup warm 2% milk (110° to 115°)
- ¼ cup plus 2 Tbsp. sugar, divided
- ½ cup butter, melted, divided
- 1 large egg, room temperature
- 1 tsp. salt
- 4 cups all-purpose flour
- 1 jar (10 oz.) seedless black raspberry preserves

SYRUP
- ⅓ cup corn syrup
- 2 Tbsp. butter, melted
- ½ tsp. vanilla extract

1. In a large bowl, dissolve yeast in warm water. Add milk, ¼ cup sugar, ¼ cup butter, egg, salt and 3½ cups flour. Beat until smooth. Stir in enough remaining flour to form a soft dough.

2. Knead on a floured surface until dough is smooth and elastic, 6-8 minutes. Place in greased bowl, turning once to grease top. Cover; let rise until doubled, about 1¼ hours.

3. Punch dough down. Turn onto a lightly floured surface; divide into 32 pieces. Flatten each piece of dough into a 3-in. disk. Place 1 tsp. preserves in center of each disk; bring edges together and seal into a rough ball.

4. Place 16 dough balls in a greased 10-in. fluted tube pan. Brush with half the remaining butter; sprinkle with 1 Tbsp. sugar. Top with remaining balls, butter and sugar. Cover; let rise until doubled, about 35 minutes. Meanwhile, preheat oven to 350°.

5. Bake until golden brown, 25-30 minutes. Combine syrup ingredients; pour over warm bread. Cool 5 minutes; invert on serving plate.

1 PIECE 274 cal., 8g fat (5g sat. fat), 34mg chol., 220mg sod., 46g carb. (18g sugars, 1g fiber), 4g pro.

Handcrafted

CREATE A FEELING OF HOME

DOMINOES

WHAT YOU'LL NEED
Five 1x6-in. boards in 6-ft. lengths
Stain
White paint
White paint marker
Polycrylic finish
Miter saw
Rag or foam brush
Paintbrush

DIRECTIONS
1. Using miter saw, cut boards into 12-in. lengths until you have 28 pieces.
2. Apply stain to pieces with rag or foam brush. Dry thoroughly.
3. Paint a white line horizontally down the center of each piece. Use white paint marker to apply appropriate dots to pieces. Dry pieces thoroughly.
4. Apply polycrylic finish to all pieces to seal. Dry thoroughly.

FLAG WREATH

WHAT YOU'LL NEED

14-in. round plastic
foam wreath form
Roughly 300 mini flag picks

DIRECTIONS

1. Lay wreath form on table or
other flat workspace.
2. Stick flag picks into wreath
form, taking care to avoid the
back, so wreath can lay flat
when hung from door. Insert
picks at varying angles to
ensure that flags are visible
from every vantage point.
3. Continue adding picks to
wreath form until plastic foam
is no longer visible.
4. Display using a wreath hanger
or hook.

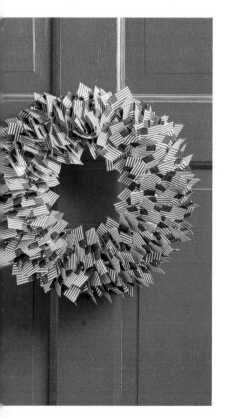

PECKING ORDER

WHAT YOU'LL NEED

Cardboard
1-in. plastic foam ball
Paint
Crepe paper
Scissors
Glue
Paintbrush

DIRECTIONS

1. Draw a hen's head and tail on
cardboard, or use the templates
at *annwoodhandmade.com
/miniature-paper-hens-free-
tutorial*.
2. Cut out and push pieces into
foam ball. Dab edges with glue.
3. Paint cardboard as desired.
4. Cut out 2 strips of crepe paper,
each 1x9 in.
5. Snip many small cuts along
1 side of each strip to create a
feathered fringe. Cut the strips
into smaller pieces.
6. Apply glue to the uncut edges
and wrap them around the ball
until only the beak and comb are
uncovered.

Autumn

Raking leaves can wait on a grand
fall afternoon, especially when
an empty swing beckons.

The Good Life

CALVES, CANE & COLLARD GREENS

Between raising cattle, working full time and harvesting sorghum
for syrup, there's never a dull moment on this fifth-generation farm

SHAYE COBB BLAIRSVILLE, GA

Hey y'all! Welcome to Nottely Oak Farms in the Appalachian Mountains of north Georgia. My husband's great-great-grandfather John Cobb established the farm in 1832 after buying a small parcel of land and then winning more acreage in the local government's land lottery.

The almost-700-acre farm stretches into North Carolina, with most of the acreage bordering the Nottely River. Once it was a dairy farm, but now my husband, Robert Cobb, and I raise feeder calves and row crops. The farm has been passed down through five generations, and we hope to pass this legacy on to our children.

Robert and I do most of the farm work, but we include our daughter, Trinity, 9, and son, Tate, 5, in all we do. They're not afraid to roll up their sleeves and help out. We also have amazing family and friends who pull together when we are cutting it close or if Robert and I just ain't enough to get the job done. We are forever grateful for their help.

If you're wondering why we need extra hands, Robert and I both hold full-time jobs off the farm. He runs equipment for a grading company; I'm a histologist at our local hospital. This means we spend evenings and weekends playing catch-up, but we wouldn't want it any other way.

WORKING THE CANE

Oct. 1 I'm usually at the hospital for work by 4 a.m., which means Robert is stuck with the morning duties of wrangling our wild animals (the kids). He can braid hair and do pigtails with the best of 'em! He goes to work after dropping them off at school and day care. This evening he finished cutting corn silage while the kids and I stripped the fodder off the sorghum cane. Around 8, we loaded up to feed the cows. Most evenings it's dark-thirty before we get to feed, but we like to do this job as a family.

Oct. 2 Stripping fodder and cutting the heads off sorghum cane by hand is a slow go, and you cannot find help to do this stuff. It ain't for the faint of heart, that is for sure. When the kids get tired of stripping fodder, they run through our collard fields. In wet years like this one, they usually return head-to-toe in mud.

After work Robert and I covered the silage pit with a tarp, which we weighed down with old tires. Any time we blow a tire or get new ones, we keep the old ones for this purpose. Let me tell you, it's no fun slinging tires that've been sitting in weeds for a year and a snake comes out on ya!

We hope to break in our brand-new hay cutter over the weekend, because we still have more than 100 acres to cut. It's been a wet year here.

Oct. 3 We usually deal strictly with Holsteins, but we just bought our first Angus calves, which have temperaments opposite to that of Holsteins. When we buy Holsteins, they have been taken from their mothers early and bottle-fed and weaned. These new Angus calves were still nursing when we got them. They're having milk withdrawal and are keeping everyone in the area awake with their bawling. Good thing our neighbors are few and far between.

Oct. 4 My dad, Donny Gibson, raked hay so Robert could start baling. We're always

so thankful for Dad's help. When we were told a month ago that he had advanced-stage cancer, it was a tough hit, but not as tough as when they told us last week that the cancer had spread—especially since we lost my mother at an early age. But Dad is tougher than nails and hasn't slowed down. He insists on helping us when he can after working all day, and he rakes hay when we've got too many irons in the fire.

Oct. 5 Today was crazy, as I had to work late. Besides work and the farm, I own a photography business, and today I had two sessions. I try to leave time to decompress after work, but today it was a rush to get the kids and make it to my first session.

Oct. 6 We expected bad weather off some incoming hurricanes, so we tried to get as much cane worked up as possible. I considered waiting a day to cut seed heads off so the cane would have a better chance at standing during the storms. But the heads hold a lot of water, and if

Left: Bandit and Scout make an appearance in the family photo with Robert, Shaye, Trinity and Tate. Above: Shaye, still in her Halloween-themed work scrubs, hurries to feed and check cattle before daylight runs out.

Left: Eager cows line up to get their fill at feeding time. Right: Collard fields provide ample space to play for Trinity and her brother, Tate.

the wind blows while they're soaked, the cane falls over—which leads to broken or tangled stalks. Either way, it makes a mess for me.

Oct. 7 We opted for a crew cab truck since I do so much work on the farm, including hauling feed. Our flatbeds are almost always hooked to the trailers—and going through the student pickup line at school with a 30-foot trailer isn't an option. Unfortunately, I needed to take my truck to the dealership to get some recalls fixed. Well, they just came back to the waiting room to tell me something happened while updating the software and they can't turn my truck off for fear of frying the system. They're loaning me a little ol' Jeep, and my truck should be ready to go tomorrow. What a week!

MAKING SYRUP FOR SORGHUM FEST

Oct. 8 We planned to pick up the first load of cane tonight, but all our friends who help us load at harvest were in the hayfields (as were we), so we postponed until Friday.

Oct. 9 Whew! It feels like we're on the 200th day of October, but it's only the ninth. I finished stripping the last bit of the second field and left to help Robert and the others load cane onto trailers. We grow sorghum for a local nonprofit that hosts

the annual Blairsville Sorghum Festival. Maybe you've heard of it if you're from this neck of the woods. The festival has been going on for more than 50 years now, and all proceeds go back into our community. It feels great to help make a difference.

Oct. 10 They just finished squeezing the cane juice from one trailer. It takes a while to hand-feed the mill, even though the boys have gotten pretty efficient. We have two fellas on the trailer loading the cane onto a platform that's even with the mill. Robert then feeds cane through the mill to squeeze all the juice from the stalks. The juice travels through three filters, which get out any seeds or other waste so the syrup is clean. Once the holding tanks are full, they light a wood fire under the pan that cooks the syrup.

A lot of sorghum-making folks use more updated methods and tools. But since we make our syrup for the festival, we strive to keep everything close to how they did it in the early days. (We even have an old mill that was operated by mules!) People who come to the festival enjoy watching this process. This year's festival was canceled due to COVID, but they're still offering up syrup for purchase.

Oct. 11 While Robert and I slung feed for the cattle, Trinity and Tate were on chicken and cat duty. I love hearing them feed the chickens—so many giggles and

little chats with the birds. We have two laying hens in particular, Waffles and Cupcake, that the kids adore, and those hens follow us all over the farm. My dad helped me make sure the nesting boxes were sturdy enough to handle the young'uns climbing on them. He was skeptical about my color choice, but the chickens and I agree that turquoise makes everything better.

THE HOME STRETCH

Oct. 15 We expected a cold front to bring temps in the low 30s, so we tried to get the cane all worked up and on the ground. I'm so excited to be in the home stretch with only one field remaining.

Oct. 16 This morning there was a crew harvesting a trailer load of collards to take down to an Atlanta farmers market. Robert got busy fluffing hay (to speed up drying time) since we hope to bale it all this week. The kids and I had a fun field day of apple picking. We got to watch pig races and take part in other activities. Then we headed to the cane field again. We plan to cook the remainder of our sorghum over the weekend, and I look forward to being able to catch my breath.

Oct. 17 There is nothing better than waking up to a brisk morning and watching the sunrise from your front porch. It's so peaceful. When the sun peeks over the mountain and its golden rays spread across the fields, it almost takes your breath away. We are truly blessed beyond what we deserve.

Oct. 18 This morning it was just coffee, two dogs and me, listening to the silence with the occasional cow hollering and rooster crowing. Scout and Bandit are blue merle Australian shepherds and two of our most cherished farmhands. Scout was a gift to my daughter almost three years ago and, let me tell you, that dog 'bout made me lose my religion. At that time I still had my old gal, Roxy, and she did not like having a puppy around. I didn't blame her—Scout was a handful. After Roxy passed away last year, it was as if Scout grew up overnight. She became one of the best dogs I've ever had. She follows hand signals and commands, and can work cattle with ease. More recently we got Bandit, who had been abused and neglected. This is his second week here. He is already learning hand signals and is such a loving dog.

Oct. 19 When we receive new cows, they each weigh around 450 pounds. We try to increase their weight by a few hundred pounds before we sell them. When they first come in, we run them through the head gate to vaccinate and worm each one. We then wait a week or so to see if any show signs of shipping fevers.

The Cobbs' front porch offers a beautiful view of their farm and forestland.

Those that do get shots. We record the tag number of the sickly cows and also mark them so we can see them in the fields. You can tell a lot about how a cow feels just by its body language and its overall behavior. A sick cow might stay away from the rest of the herd, standing with its head down. And then there are the telltale signs of coughing and secreting mucus.

Oct. 20 The kids and I fed the herd a little early tonight as Robert was baling the last bit of hay. We'd expected around 2,000 round bales for the year, and although the fickle weather has hindered us, we are thankful for the yield we got.

Oct. 21 Y'all, today was the day ... the last day of the season in the cane field! This year has been tough. We couldn't hardly find people to help, which made the whole process feel drawn out. We finally finished with the cane about 6 p.m.

DANCING IT UP
Oct. 23 All the good folks that volunteer at the Blairsville Sorghum Festival came to help load our cane. We ended up with 2½ trailer loads. They'll cook it tomorrow starting at first light; meanwhile I'll be cooking up a storm for our annual Halloween shindig.

I went a little overboard this year, since all the Halloween festivities in our town are canceled because of the pandemic. I built a *piñata* and Trinity filled it with goodies. I also made three varieties of chili: mild, spicy and white chicken. I plan to finish the kids' costumes tonight. Every year I try my best at making the kids' visions come to life. This year Trinity wanted to be a zombie four-wheeler racer, complete with a bone protruding from her leg. Tate wanted to dress like his daddy and be a track hoe operator, complete with working lights.

Oct. 24 Tate's costume came out awesome—I made it with a working bucket arm and headlights. It lasted all of an hour because as soon as I turned my back that boy was out the door, trying to dig holes in the yard with it. Trinity's costume was also a hit. She even got on her four-wheeler and did a lap around the barn so her hair would look windblown.

The last guests left our Halloween party at about 2 a.m. It was a great turnout and we had the best time! The kids (and maybe some adults) had a pumpkin-guts fight, and there are still pumpkin guts everywhere.

Oct. 25 We ended up with a few hundred gallons of sorghum syrup. Each year it is hard work day in and day out, but the reward is worth it.

Today we helped our friend Brock Kelly run his sorghum through the mill. Most years, after the last day at the mill, we hold a meal and a town square dance where everyone can unwind and cut a rug. This is my husband's favorite part! When we first started courting, he tried to talk me into going to one of the dances, but I was reluctant. Well, he finally convinced me to go and that was all she wrote. We haven't missed one since, except this year, when they had to cancel all of the dances because of COVID-19. There is always next year, Lord willing.

The new cattle aren't used to us quite yet, so tonight we had to herd them to the feed troughs. Robert always uses our Polaris Ranger, but I prefer walking with the dogs. We had a few cows across the creek that needed to be pushed toward the far end of the field. I had my mucks on, so Scout and I went to get them. I looked back at Robert and saw we had a calf stuck in the creek. This fella must've struggled all morning to get up that creek bank and was just plum tuckered out. He was lying partly in the creek and partly on the bank. Bless his heart, he couldn't get traction to get up the bank; we'd just had rain and our Georgia clay was slicker than dog poop.

Did I mention the calf was in the deepest section of the creek? And that muck boots are great at keeping water out until the water is so deep it flows over the tops of the boots? Let me tell you, these mountain creeks are cold! We soon figured out we couldn't move that 800-pound fella by hand, so Robert went for the tractor while Scout and I herded the rest of the cattle to the other side of the field. With each step I took, water shot out the tops of my mucks.

Oct. 26 We got in a few newly weaned Holsteins—the cutest little things! As Robert and I worked some of them this evening, one ran into a barn stall instead of out to the field. I went to run him out and his body language changed, so I knew I needed to hurry on out of there and fast. Sure enough, the bull started after me, but I got behind the fence before he reached me. I could sign up to be a rodeo clown.

Oct. 30 We had planned a quick family getaway to Pigeon Forge, Tennessee, but we have bulls due to arrive, plus we're getting a feed delivery in the morning. I had already booked our stay—at a place doing a Halloween festival for kids—so just Trinity, Tate and I left after I got off work. That night I talked to Robert and he said the farm was looking good, considering the weather. Cold one minute, hot the next.

Postscript: Between the pandemic, the unpredictable weather and Dad's health, October 2020 was a roller-coaster ride. But by 2021 Dad was doing better— his treatments slowed progression of the disease, which we were thankful for. It was a challenging season, but farming is always challenging. We hoped to resume a sense of normalcy for the sorghum season in subsequent years, and we looked forward to once again joining our community to celebrate autumn at the sorghum festival here in Blairsville, Georgia.

Robert, driving a Massey Ferguson, cuts corn silage. Once he has a full load, it'll be driven to the silage pit and covered for safe storage.

WHERE THE TALL CORN GROWS

Raising Iowa's No. 1 crop—plus soybeans and swine—
keeps this farm family moving

CRISTEN CLARK RUNNELLS, IA

Hi! My name is Cristen Clark. I'm a sixth-generation Iowa farmer with a passion for cooking, working with my family and coaching youth sports (including softball pitching). My great-great-great-grandfather settled this farm in 1869, and it has been in our family ever since. I work on the farm with my dad, Rodger Slings, and my husband, Mike Clark. Mike and I also run a butcher pig business. If I'm not on the farm, you'll find me developing recipes, playing with pigs or pulling weeds.

I'm a food editor for *Our Iowa* magazine and write about recipes and cooking for other publications as well. I stay busy as an ambassador for the Iowa Food and Family Project, which connects consumers with farmers in my state, and I have a blog called Food & Swine, where I share contest-winning recipes and stories from our farm. Finally, I run a project called Owned and Bred, which celebrates people from Polk County who raise their own pigs for the county fair.

BREEDING, BLOGGING & CAMPING

Oct. 1 Fall is my favorite time of year. Typically in October we're harvesting soybeans or corn, and at the end of the month we like to visit apple orchards and pumpkin patches. This year was unseasonably wet, so we got an awfully late start on harvest. It's been nerve-wracking to sit by and wait for Mother Nature to provide us with drier weather.

It's peak breeding season, and many of our show-type sows were bred to various boars, so we'll have plenty of pigs for area youth to select for fairs and national shows.

On my blog, I write about modern farming practices and share recipes that feature pork. Today I joined some folks from Iowa Pork Producers to visit Mi Patria, a restaurant in Des Moines, to learn and write about the menu. I sat with Cesar, the owner and head chef, and heard about his family's path to starting the only Ecuadorian restaurant in Central Iowa. In addition to being the chef, Cesar buses tables, does dishes and greets diners. My favorite dish was the *hornado con mote*. It showcases brilliantly flavored pulled pork on a bed of rice with hominy and a potato cake. It was garnished with a bright salad called *ensalada criolla*.

Oct. 2 Yet another wet day. Ick! People are getting edgy. I wonder if we'll ever be able to start harvest.

Oct. 3 Last year I renovated an older

> *We picked corn at a location where the hills are so steep that when I drive across them, I find myself lifting my leg up in the air to feel more centered.*

fifth-wheel camper. I painted, replaced old flooring, updated the furnishings and made a reading nook for the kids. This enabled us to make last-minute plans to go camping this weekend with friends.

Oct. 4 Last night Mike and I set up the camper, then we checked on the pigs we have on feed. I pulled the kids out of school early to get a jump-start on the weekend. At camp, we played bag toss and bocce ball while waiting for our friends. It's always so nice to be out in the woods with a campfire going and leaves beginning to turn. We had soup for supper and the kids made s'mores. The warm evening turned chilly, so we heated the camper with a space heater.

Oct. 5 We can't get too far away from the farm when we camp. The pigs, which

Left: Cristen and Mike Clark with their children, Halle and Barrett. Above: Keep up with the Clark family and find recipes and more farm photos by visiting Cristen's blog at *foodandswine.com*.

At the farm pond, Mike teaches Barrett the finer points of fishing.

Oct. 8 We were rained out again today so our list of accomplishments was short: just a little greasing and washing the windows of our rigs in anticipation of getting into the field.

Oct. 9 Today I joined bloggers from all over the U.S. on a tour of modern pork production facilities. I never miss a chance to engage with people who aren't "farm-iliar." There is much to be learned from those who want to know more about how food is grown and raised. Dinners, tours and other activities are good platforms for communicating with people who will share that info with audiences from coast to coast.

Oct. 11 Yesterday Mike started shipping hogs from our commercial site. Today there was more rain. I'm beginning to think we're never going to get this crop out of the ground.

Oct. 12 We anticipated picking some corn in the afternoon. If not today, we thought, then definitely tomorrow. Moisture is above 20%, but paying a drying bill is better than waiting until spring to pick the corn.

Oct. 13 We picked corn all day, and yields were good. It felt so nice to be productive and unhindered by rain, but catching corn on the go and unloading it got the best of me. I put Tiger Balm on my neck and it helped—along with the occasional ibuprofen.

Oct. 14 It was cold when I got up, so I made soup. I had veggies to use up and, of course, some ham. I made more than enough—plenty to bring out to the field. It is such a comfort to eat a hot meal in the field when so often lunch consists of a sandwich made with cold cuts.

include purebred breeding stock, need to be checked a few times a day. Mike went home in the morning and evening to do chores, look over everything, and water, feed and exercise our dog, Lady. At home she has free run of the place and a pond she swims in daily. Our friend Grace comes to check on her in the afternoons when we're gone.

PICKING CORN—FINALLY!

Oct. 7 Returned home to find the earth totally soaked. We can't harvest corn until it warms up and we get some wind to dry things out, but the combine is greased and ready to go. My mom, Ceil Slings, made field snacks. Her famous mixture includes peanuts, M&Ms and candy corn. Barrett likes candy corn and Halle likes peanuts, so I get the M&Ms all to myself when they ride along.

PIGS ON THE LOOSE

Oct. 15 We cut beans at my late Grandma Madeline's farm yesterday and at a second field nearby. Today my dad took a few loads to town while I washed tractors and combine windows. My hands were freezing, but it's nice to see a little better from the cab. I also buffed all the grit off the hazard lights so we can safely move through town. I left early for parent-teacher conferences, and the kids seem to be doing well at school.

Oct. 16 On this day 11 years ago I was roaring through a field full of tile ditches on an ATV. I must have had a bumpy ride because the next day I had Halle—two weeks early! Every so often we're done harvesting by this time and we go out for her birthday dinner. This year we'll be having pizza in the field.

The power-washing crew washed our commercial site so it would be clean for the pigs coming in a week.

Oct. 17 Dad made sure I didn't have to be in the field much because my niece Kemper is sick. (She ended up in the hospital with pneumonia.) Since "Big Sis" was sick, I babysat her sister, Kendyl. My kids got out of school early, and we made crafts and ate dinner at Halle's favorite place. I kept Kendyl with us and she had a great time with her cousins.

Oct. 18 Pigs got out! The kids and I had to round up 120-pound boars that had popped their gate open. Later I helped Dad move the tractors and combine to a field across town. The beans were damp but doable—good, since they need to come out before the next rain.

Oct. 19 It rained all morning so I took Kendyl to visit Kemper in the hospital. She was improving, but it's so scary to see a healthy kid so sick.

Oct. 20 It rained 1.2 inches. I never thought I'd be thankful for rain during a wet harvest, but I'm sick, and being in a bouncy tractor seat with a head cold is no fun.

Oct. 21 I feel awful, but with a few bursts of energy, I managed to clean and to do laundry. It doesn't sound like much, but having a clean house at the end of a long harvest day makes going to bed easier.

LONG LINES AT THE CO-OP

Oct. 22 Today we picked corn at the farm of the late Bob Jennings. His daughter Janice rode along, and we were able to visit for a while. She told me how lucky I am to be able to work alongside my dad, and we had a nice time sharing stories of her father. I left with enough time to get my car and take Halle to a gym in Ankeny by 8:30 p.m. Once I got to my car, though,

When unseasonable amounts of rain delay the harvest, the work can sometimes stretch well into evening hours.

Cristen's dad, Rodger, shares some farming wisdom with the next generation of Clarks.

the fuel light came on. I think Halle and I glided into the gym parking lot on fumes. I helped Dad fuel all of the machines today but clearly I forgot my own!

Oct. 24 Kendyl rode along to pick corn at my late grandma's farm. She brought a lunch box and a cozy blanket to wrap up in for her nap. Since the field is nice and flat, I let her sit on my lap and drive a bit. She hopped on the radio to give Grandpa Rodger a hard time. He just laughed. It was a nice distraction—we're all scared about how sick her sister is.

Oct. 25 Things are drying out enough to cut soybeans. I visited Kemper today and Dad cut soybeans by himself. Mike vaccinated pigs.

Oct. 26 I helped Dad get the machinery set at the first field and delivered field lunches. Then I drove to the hospital to sit with my sister.

Oct. 27 We picked corn at a location where the hills are so steep that when I

drive across them, I find myself lifting my leg up in the air to feel more centered. The grain tank sensor was acting up, so once Dad's combine was empty, we shut it down and I climbed into the tank. I saw that a piece of the sensor arm was crimped badly and corn was wedged so that it disturbed the sensor's function. Happily, the problem was easy to fix.

The co-op is starting to slow. Everyone is catching up, so lots of wet corn is hitting the facility at the same time. We looked for storage at the next fields to be picked, and I'm pretty sure Dad has it figured out so we can get more corn picked before the upcoming snow. Wow ... snow.

Oct. 28 We finished the hilly field, but the lines at the co-op are worse than yesterday. There aren't enough dryers to handle all the wet corn. We checked cows, ate lunch and waited. Still, nothing. So we emptied the combine and moved home to start corn there. Then the grain tank sensor failed again. It snowed from evening till morning. I called Dad before bed to get my marching orders: "Take the day off."

Oct. 29 I took the kids to school and called Dad before going home to do office work. He asked what I was doing, to which I said, "Nothing," and I ended up going over to help with various chores. So much for a day off! Mike unloaded the next set of pigs at the commercial site today.

Oct. 30 We picked corn at home, where we have plenty of grain bin storage so we won't have to take it to town and wait in the lines, thank goodness. The work gets monotonous, so sometimes I make a game out of it to see if I can get back in time before my previous load is emptied into the bins. I get a load, drag it in, unload it onto the wagon, turn on the old Farmall M and grain auger, and head back out for another load.

Help came in the late afternoon so I took my kids to the hospital to join Kemper for the pediatric trick-or-treat event. Kemper dressed up as Wonder Woman, and we wheeled her IV stand beside her as she went around collecting treats and handing out bracelets, candy and pencils to other patients and staff. She was accompanied by her surgeon and other doctors and nurses to make sure the trip went smoothly. They were dressed like characters from the movie *Frozen*, which she loves. After the 45-minute parade through the hospital, she was tuckered out.

Oct. 31 More snow. No field work could be done today. It was really cold outside so I worked on some magazine columns and newsletters that are due late next week. Mike vaccinated the second set of pigs that just arrived at the commercial site.

Postscript: Things really changed since I wrote this diary in 2019! Our kids, Halle and Barrett, are older. The pandemic hit just before a busy summer of pig shows and sports was set to begin, so we spent the warm months camping all around central Iowa. It was nice to slow down and enjoy each other's company, play games, ride bikes and have campfires.

The pig business picked up at the height of the shutdowns. Lots of people wanted to fill their freezers with local pork, and we were happy to help! We could hardly meet the demand for our Durocs, but we are thankful for our new customers and they've stuck with us.

One nice surprise was receiving the Iowa 4-H Legacy Award for a Distinguished Alumni this year. I was so honored! 4-H does great things for kids and gives us so many tools to carry forward.

Looking ahead, we hope to keep up some of the slowdown the pandemic years have shown us. We notched out several small vacations, and are always eager to hike, see wildlife and enjoy the scenery of different states!

Halle offers feed to a few of the Durocs.

INTANGIBLE REWARDS

One tractor united two farmers
and three generations

TOM O'CONNOR NEW LENOX, IL

My neighbor Lloyd Brandau was a lifelong farmer and a proud veteran of the Korean conflict. He had an original, unrestored 1958 John Deere 620. When the time came to have it painted, he reached out to me. I agreed to do the work under one condition: Lloyd could pay for the paint and parts, but my labor would be considered a gift. I admired Lloyd—he was one of a kind. He loved his life and enjoyed each day, and he made everyone around him feel the same.

Lloyd was spending the winter in Arizona with his wife, Marilyn Brandau, when I started to work on his John Deere. My son, Tommy, had just graduated from college and was living on our farmstead while finishing an internship, so not only was he around to help, but I had the chance to teach him how to paint a tractor.

Tommy and I had a great time taking apart and fixing the 620. It was a good bonding experience, and I chronicled the teardown process by taking lots of photos. The days and weeks were clicking by, and after we had painted everything, we started to reassemble it. The project took about 65 days and some nights to complete. Most of what I wanted to buy new, such as the steering wheel, tires, decals, emblems and seat, were readily available on the internet.

When we finished, I composed a letter to Lloyd, including an itemized list of parts and materials but reminding him of our initial agreement—that I would not accept payment for my labor. When one of his sons went to visit in Arizona, I asked him to take along a book of restoration photos.

Lloyd responded with a letter and the full payment for parts. He respected my wishes, he said, but added, "I agreed to not pay you for your labor, but you never said I couldn't pay your son." I called Lloyd to thank him. I told him I would give Tommy a small amount of the money now and put the rest into his savings so that he might benefit for years to come. Lloyd liked this plan.

Tommy and I gave the finished tractor to Lloyd when he and Marilyn returned home. He loved it and expressed his thanks. I told him I thought I'd gotten more out of the project than he had. And we both knew I wasn't talking about anything tangible.

POULTRY ROYALTY

Sharing a passion for poultry is her crowning achievement

EMMA WEEKS CHIPLEY, FL

Why did the chicken cross the road? To get to my house, of course! As an 11-year-old, I realize I'm barely out of the hatchling stage, but boy, I can tell you a lot about chickens. They're kind of my thing!

I joined the local 4-H livestock club when I was 8, and my first project was the Chick Chain, which teaches kids how to raise chicks into hens. After a few meetings, I picked up my new chicks. I soon knew this was something I would stick with. My chicks claimed half our property. And I have fallen in love with raising chickens and everything that comes along with it!

This project is tons of fun, but it has also given me the opportunity to become an entrepreneur. I started out selling the eggs to family and friends, and before long I developed an interest in rare and critically endangered breeds. I currently have about eight flocks consisting of Ayam Cemanis, blue Jersey Giants, standard Blue Laced Red Wyandottes, red-shouldered Yokohamas and Golden Cuckoo Marans. I am also developing a homegrown line of White Marans.

My mom publicizes our birds on social media, and my dad created a website. Through these avenues, we share my flocks and offer their fertilized eggs to others. I ship eggs all over the United States for fellow poultry enthusiasts to hatch in their own incubators. It's a big thrill to know that my hens have "chick children" in almost every single state! I can't wait to see how my business grows.

I love creating educational poultry exhibits with my family for local and state fairs—and in addition to competing in poultry and livestock judging events, I enjoy showing my birds as a pageant participant.

In 2020, I earned the title of Junior Miss Northwest Florida. I take this title and job seriously, and it has given me the perfect stage to share my passion for poultry with others my age. My pageant sisters affectionately call me Chicken Girl.

I recently created a platform called the Eden Project to help provide information about 4-H in our community and state. I aspire to inspire. And who knows? Maybe it will bring someone else as much joy as it brings me.

In the years since then-8-year-old Emma joined the 4-H livestock club, rare and endangered chicken breeds have come to rule the roost at the Weeks home.

Scrapbook

CAPTURE THE BEAUTY AROUND YOU

1. SUCH A TREAT

Lucy is the youngest of our five children. She stood there talking to that horse about trick-or-treating for the longest time—it's one of our favorite fall pictures.

KATIE BARR KESWICK, VA

2. TIME FOR A NAP

It was such an honor to watch this barred owl all afternoon in a tree behind my fence. It didn't seem to mind me at all, as you can see by its big yawn between preening times.

JENNIFER RUSH GRESHAM, OR

1

1. STILL STANDING

While traveling through Texas, we discovered the Fort Griffin State Historic Site in Albany, Texas. Built in 1867, it was once home to more than 465 soldiers, officers, their families and other civilians. At its peak there were more than 60 buildings on the site, but only six were completely constructed out of stone. My favorite was this one, Sutler's Store.

KELLIE CARTER NEWCASTLE, OK

2. SNACK BOWL

Blue jays showed up in my backyard regularly after I filled this little pumpkin with seeds.

VICTORIA SCHWINABART SWANTON, MD

3. TRAIL STOP

This is one of my favorite spots on the Shingle Mill Pathway in Michigan's Pigeon River Country State Forest.

JIM HANUS RICHMOND, MI

1. GOURDS 'N' GRANDKIDS

My husband's brother plants pumpkins at our farm every year, and he always needs help harvesting. Our crew usually consists of the adults and quite a few grandchildren.

DAWN GREEN GRAND MOUND, IA

2. FLUFFY FRIEND

An adorable tufted titmouse enjoyed some corn at a feeding station in Dorothy Carnes County Park near Fort Atkinson, Wisconsin. I don't have titmice at my own feeders very often, so I was thrilled to spend some time with this little cutie.

BARBARA HOULIHAN MADISON, WI

3. PERFECTLY POSED

I was traveling down the road one day and saw this gorgeous eagle surrounded by fall colors. I had to pull over and snap a photo.

SHERRY SANDERS MOUNTAIN HOME, AR

TRANQUIL WATERS
Mountain Fork River in Beavers
Bend State Park near Broken Bow,
Oklahoma, lights up in the late
afternoon. During one visit, I spotted
a lone fisherman amid the glowing
foliage, reflected in the glassy water.

CAROLYN FLETCHER MASON CITY, IA

1. TINY TRACTOR TALK

My 2-year-old, Breelyn, loves playing on this old pedal tractor. Her dad, Rudin, got it for Christmas when he was a kid. When he found it years later at his parents' farm, he restored it for our kids.

MEGHAN EMBORSKY SALAMANCA, NY

2. HARVEST HELPERS

My daughters Elle and Emma love to help Papa and Amma (my dad and mom) on the farm. The girls think it's a disaster if Papa spills a few beans or a little corn! They had fun playing farmers on a warm October day in central Illinois.

JILL BURKOWSKI ROSSVILLE, IL

3. TURKEY TROT

I took this picture in the fall at Shenandoah National Park in Virginia. As I was driving through the park, I noticed Ms. Turkey running toward me down a stone wall. It was such an amazing moment.

RON SPRATT NOTTINGHAM, MD

1. JUST DUCKY

I saw a group of wood ducks feeding in a forest pond. They were taking turns flying off and exercising their wings, showing off their deep, rich colors.

DOUGLAS BEALL CAMP SHERMAN, OR

2. PRIDE AND JOY

John Tanner shows off his grandson, Tanner, and his barn quilt. He is very proud of both! He constructed and installed the quilt himself, and he lights it up at night so passersby can get a good view.

GERALDINE TANNER CHILLICOTHE, OH

3. WATER FEATURE

We took a driving trip from Michigan through the Dakotas to Wyoming, stopping at some places we had not visited before. In the Black Hills of South Dakota, we came across Spearfish Falls in a very pretty setting with nice color.

ROY GOLDSBERRY ROCHESTER HILLS, MI

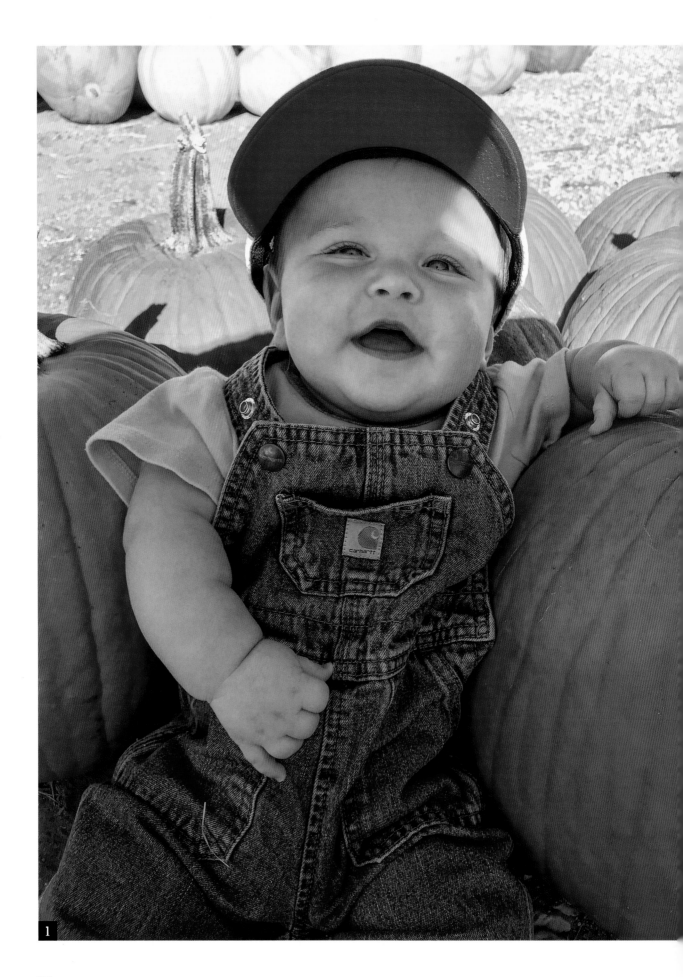

1. PATCH PERFECT
Thurman Joe Hiskett, aka Little T, was born two months early in March. We are so blessed to celebrate every fall season with our little bull.

JENNY HISKETT FALLON, NV

2. CLOSE ENCOUNTERS
This is a favorite picture of mine. It's my mom with our friendly alpaca, named Kimbo. She enjoys visiting with him.

WENDY S. BEATTY CLEAR BROOK, VA

3. TEA FOR TWO (OR THREE)
Briley, 6, serves a spot of "tea" to Meghan, 4, who isn't impressed with the bug she found in her cup.

KIRSTEN BERGER FRIENDSHIP, WI

1. SERENE SCENERY

While motorcycling in Wisconsin's North Woods, I searched out quiet country back roads. I came across small, peaceful Bradley Park in the town of Tomahawk.

KENNY ROSZAK MILWAUKEE, WI

2. NATURE'S GIFT

Near North Carolina's Pisgah National Forest, I found Looking Glass Falls. I braved the rocky climb down to get to the best vantage point.

LUCY SULLIVAN OCALA, FL

3. ROLLING WITH IT

I love it when my littles want to help out around the farm, even if their ambitions sometimes outweigh their abilities!

MARGIE LYTLE WASILLA, AK

Heart & Soul

A PINCH OF CARE

Baking as a family takes time—but the togetherness brings sweet rewards

VALERIE CHAMBERLAIN RENFREW, ON

T he old kitchen table rattles as Molly kneads and folds, turns and presses, flips and flops the soft mound of dough in a dusting of flour. She pats it into a perfect circle and smiles. Brushing the flour from her hands, Molly moves on to prep the bread pans. She knows how to grease and flour them just so, tapping the pans from end to end to form a coating, letting the excess flour fall.

It doesn't seem so long ago that this same girl was 3 years old, tugging on my shirt and asking, "Mommy, I help?" I knew it would take me twice as long, but I tied aprons on my kids when they were tall enough to stand on chairs and peer into the big mixing bowls on the kitchen counter. I measured and they poured. They stuck their little fingers in the bowl when they thought I didn't see. They talked my ear off, making me lose my place in the recipe. They each held a big spoon in their tiny hands and stirred five whole circles before surrendering the task back to my stronger arms. The process took longer, but many sweet conversations took place while we made delicious treats.

I admit I sometimes lost patience and sent the cherubs on their way. Cookies burned while I was busy wiping sticky fingers, and the muffins weren't always light and fluffy. Yet each time we gathered at the counter, I shared my love and gave them the gift of time, slowness and care.

These days, my kids are doing it all. They make chocolate chip cookies, brownies and gingersnaps, to name a few. Molly, in particular, has grown fond of baking bread. Eating it, too. She follows a simple,

They stuck their little fingers in the bowl when they thought I didn't see.

well-loved, handwritten recipe that's big enough to produce two loaves. She adores the whole process, from measuring and mixing straight through to lifting the golden loaves from the oven.

My husband and I secretly discussed getting Molly a bread machine for her next birthday. She could pour in the ingredients, press a few buttons and walk away! We thought we were geniuses for a whole five minutes. That's how long it took us to realize what we would be taking away from her. She loves the feeling of the flour in her hands and the smooth stretch of dough when she's kneading it. One of her favorite parts is punching the dough down after it has risen, all puffy, in a giant bowl resting over the warm air vent.

She knows she needs about half a day to get through the process, and she willingly sets aside the time. We decided to let her take that time, and we enjoy the end result when she offers slices of fresh, warm bread. Pass the butter, please.

At 14, Molly developed a fondness for making bread from scratch.

THE SWING

Life changed, but one woman found constant comfort in the steady sway of a safe place to sit

DIANE SHREWSBERRY PADUCAH, KY

When I was a child, the porch swing at my grandparents' home faced the creek. The sunset was always lovely there, in the swing.

My grandmother used to sit in her rocker beside me and tell me tales of folklore that I never tired of hearing. As night progressed, frogs called, and the whippoorwill brought in the dusk. The creak of the swing lulled me to sleep.

Soon adulthood was upon me, and I married a soldier. I had a swing in the front yard of my first home. It was on the farm where I grew up, and I would sit in the swing with a baby at my feet, awaiting the mail and feeling the anticipation of perhaps a letter from Vietnam.

Weary of days with no word and filled with worry of "what-ifs," I let the swing help me solve my problems. Back-and-

forth ... days of disappointment mixed with days of content as I reread a letter giving me hope and strength.

Things change, but the swing was my constant, lulling all my children to sleep. I would bundle up and retreat to the swing during the cold winters to breathe fresh air. When my life began to unravel and I realized I would go through a divorce, I retreated to the swing. Dark days followed; hard decisions were made, all in the easy back-and-forth of the swing.

I remarried and moved to a new home with bright hopes and happy thoughts, immediately installing a swing on an oak tree in the backyard.

Time creases my face, and the slats in my swing are weathered as well. I take a few moments each day to reflect, reminisce and enjoy my forever friend—the swing.

LEARNING FROM LITTLE RED

Her dad—and his truck—offered lessons that'll endure longer than any engine

HANNAH ROTH WICHITA, KS

Inside my folks' garage is a 1986 Nissan pickup named Little Red that my dad has owned for more than 30 years. He gives it excellent care, so my mom, my sister and I refer to it as his baby. Little Red is part of so many good memories—and important lessons, too.

My dad and his pickup taught me about service. After every big storm, there was my dad in his truck with a chainsaw, ready to lend a hand. When we had a snow, Dad maneuvered through the drifts because "Ms. Martin up the road probably needs her driveway shoveled." I tagged along and, at times, wished Dad wasn't such a perfectionist so we could just go home already. But I learned that part of service is getting the job done right.

My dad and his pickup taught me about patience. I have never liked fishing, but my family enjoys it, so I'd always get dragged along. We'd load up the pickup and drive out to the lake or to the ponds in the pasture near our house. I was ready to move on after 10 minutes. But Dad would always convince me to stick it out. "You can't get everything you want right away," he'd say. I'd roll my eyes and cast my line into yet another tree, but eventually I learned that the greatest rewards take time.

My dad and his pickup taught me about hard work. Even on his days off, Dad was hard at it, hauling the project of the day. I was often by his side, complaining about a perfectly good Saturday gone to waste. But now I am grateful to have learned discipline and how to accomplish things on time.

My dad and his pickup taught me about caring for others. Sometimes on Sunday afternoons I'd see him driving off in Little Red to visit an older man who didn't get out much. A few times I went with him, and by doing so I got to know one of the most fascinating storytellers I have ever met. These visits taught me that people are more important than to-do lists.

My dad and his pickup taught me about contentment and sacrifice. "You do the best you can with what you have," he says. Little Red has its share of issues. It starts on the third try, if you're lucky. Yet Dad plans to use it for as long as it runs. When I wanted a new car, Dad advised me to save up rather than taking on debt.

One of these days Little Red won't start on the third, the fourth or even the 100th try, but I will carry its lessons—and my dad's—well into the future.

Taste of the Country

1. In a small bowl, mix egg yolk with ¼ cup ice water; set aside. Place flour, sugar and salt in a food processor; pulse until blended. Add shortening and butter; pulse until shortening and butter are the size of peas. While pulsing, add egg yolk mixture. Add just enough of the remaining ice water to form moist crumbs. Divide dough in half. Shape each into a disk; wrap and refrigerate 1 hour or overnight.

2. Preheat oven to 400°. Scrub sweet potatoes; place in a 13x9-in. baking pan with 1½ cups water. Bake until tender, 45-50 minutes. Meanwhile, on a lightly floured surface, roll 1 disk of dough into a ⅛-in.-thick circle; transfer to a 9-in. deep-dish pie plate. Trim crust to ½ in. beyond rim of plate; flute edge. Roll remaining disk to ⅛-in. thickness; cut into desired shapes with floured 1-in. cookie cutters. Place on a parchment-lined baking sheet. Refrigerate crust and cutouts for at least 30 minutes.

3. Peel sweet potatoes when cool enough to handle; place in a food processor. Pulse to coarsely mash. Add brown sugar and next 8 ingredients; blend until smooth. Pour filling into chilled crust. Bake on lowest oven rack for 15 minutes. Reduce oven setting to 350°; bake until center is just set, 20-25 minutes. Bake crust cutouts on upper oven rack until golden brown, 10-12 minutes. Cool on a wire rack; decorate pie with cutouts and additional toppings as desired.

1 PIECE 726 cal., 37g fat (18g sat. fat), 147mg chol., 500mg sod., 88g carb. (38g sugars, 6g fiber), 10g pro.

THE BEST SWEET POTATO PIE

PREP 1½ hours + chilling
BAKE 35 min. + cooling
MAKES 8 servings

CRUST

1	large egg yolk
¼	to ½ cup ice water, divided
2½	cups all-purpose flour
3	Tbsp. sugar
½	tsp. salt
½	cup cold shortening, cubed
½	cup cold butter, cubed

FILLING

2½	lbs. sweet potatoes
⅔	cup packed brown sugar
½	cup sour cream
3	large eggs, lightly beaten
⅓	cup butter, melted
1	Tbsp. bourbon
2	tsp. vanilla extract
1½	tsp. ground cinnamon
½	tsp. ground nutmeg
½	tsp. salt

Optional toppings: Whipped cream and sugared cranberries

FLUFFY CARAMEL APPLE DIP

TAKES 30 min. **MAKES** 2 cups

- 1 pkg. (8 oz.) cream cheese, softened
- ½ cup packed brown sugar
- ¼ cup caramel ice cream topping
- 1 tsp. vanilla extract
- 1 cup marshmallow creme
  Apple slices

In a small bowl, beat cream cheese, brown sugar, caramel topping and vanilla until smooth; fold in marshmallow creme. Serve with apple slices.

2 TBSP. 110 cal., 5g fat (3g sat. fat), 14mg chol., 69mg sod., 15g carb. (14g sugars, 0 fiber), 1g pro.

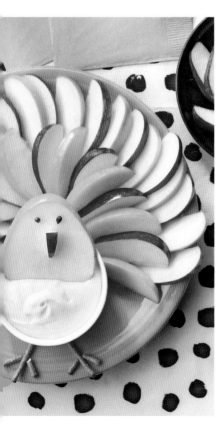

JACK-O'-LANTERN EMPANADAS

PREP 45 min. **BAKE:** 15 min.
MAKES 2½ dozen

- 1 Tbsp. canola oil
- ½ cup frozen corn
- ¼ cup finely chopped onion
- ¼ cup finely chopped sweet red pepper
- 2 garlic cloves, minced
- 1 can (15 oz.) pumpkin
- ½ cup black beans, rinsed and drained
- 2 tsp. chili powder
- ¾ tsp. salt
- ¾ tsp. ground cumin
- ½ tsp. dried oregano
- 2 pkg. (14.1 oz. each) refrigerated pie crust
- 1 large egg
- 1 Tbsp. water

1. Preheat oven to 425°. In a skillet, heat oil over medium heat. Add corn, onion and red pepper; cook until tender, 2-3 minutes. Add garlic; cook 1 minute longer. Add pumpkin, beans and seasonings; heat through. Cool slightly.

2. On a lightly floured surface, unroll pie crust. Cut 60 pumpkins with a 3-in. floured pumpkin-shaped or round cookie cutter, rerolling crust as necessary. Place half the cutouts 2 in. apart on parchment-lined baking sheets; top each with about 1 Tbsp. pumpkin mixture. Using a knife, cut jack-o'-lantern faces out of remaining cutouts. Place over pumpkin mixture; press the edges to seal.

3. In a small bowl, whisk egg and water; brush over empanadas. Bake until golden brown, 12-15 minutes. Remove from pan to wire racks.

1 EMPANADA 137 cal., 8g fat (3g sat. fat), 11mg chol., 174mg sod., 15g carb. (2g sugars, 1g fiber), 2g pro.

CREAMY CHICKEN NOODLE STEW

TAKES 30 min. **MAKES** 8 servings (2 qt.)

- ⅓ cup butter, cubed
- 1 medium carrot, shredded
- 1 celery rib, finely chopped
- ⅓ cup all-purpose flour
- 1 carton (32 oz.) chicken broth
- ½ cup half-and-half cream
- ½ cup 2% milk
- 1 cup uncooked kluski or other egg noodles
- 2 cups cubed cooked chicken
- 1½ cups shredded cheddar cheese
- ¼ tsp. salt
- ¼ tsp. pepper

1. In a large saucepan, heat butter over medium-high heat; saute carrot and celery until tender, 3-5 minutes. Stir in flour until blended; gradually add broth, cream and milk. Bring to a boil, stirring constantly; cook and stir until thickened, 1-2 minutes.

2. Stir in noodles. Reduce heat; simmer, uncovered, until noodles are al dente, 7-10 minutes, stirring occasionally. Add the remaining ingredients; cook and stir until chicken is heated through and cheese is melted.

1 CUP 285 cal., 18g fat (11g sat. fat), 92mg chol., 823mg sod., 11g carb. (2g sugars, 1g fiber), 18g pro.

WHOLE WHEAT BREAD

PREP 20 min. + rising **BAKE** 40 min.
MAKES 2 loaves (16 pieces each)

- 1 pkg. (¼ oz.) active dry yeast
- 3 cups warm water (110° to 115°), divided
- ¾ cup canola oil
- ¼ cup sugar
- ¼ cup molasses
- 1 Tbsp. salt
- 7 to 7½ cups all-purpose flour
- 3 cups whole wheat flour

1. In a large bowl, dissolve yeast in ¾ cup warm water. Add oil, sugar, molasses, salt and remaining water. Combine flours; add 4-5 cups flour to mixture. Beat until smooth. Add enough remaining flour to form a firm dough.

2. Turn onto a lightly floured surface; knead until smooth and elastic, 6-8 minutes. Place in a greased bowl, turning once to grease top. Cover and let rise in a warm place until doubled, about 1 hour.

3. Punch dough down. Turn onto a lightly floured surface; divide in half. Shape each portion into a loaf. Place in 2 greased 9x5-in. loaf pans. Cover and let rise until doubled, about 30 minutes.

4. Preheat oven to 350°. Bake loaves until golden brown, 40-45 minutes. Remove from pans to cool on wire racks.

1 PIECE 168 cal., 6g fat (1g sat. fat), 0 chol., 223mg sod., 26g carb. (4g sugars, 2g fiber), 4g pro.

CRANBERRY-APPLE LATTICE PIE

PREP 40 min. + chilling
BAKE 65 min. + cooling
MAKES 8 servings

CRUST

2½	cups all-purpose flour
1	Tbsp. sugar
¾	tsp. salt
½	cup cold unsalted butter, cubed
⅓	cup cold shortening
5	to 7 Tbsp. ice water

FILLING

½	cup dried currants or raisins
2	Tbsp. dark rum or water
1	cup fresh or frozen cranberries, divided
¾	cup sugar, divided
6	medium baking apples, such as Fuji or Braeburn (about 2 lbs.), peeled and cut into ¼-in. slices
2	Tbsp. quick-cooking tapioca
1	Tbsp. lemon juice
2	tsp. grated lemon zest
½	tsp. ground cinnamon

EGG WASH

2	tsp. sugar
	Dash ground cinnamon
1	large egg
1	Tbsp. 2% milk or heavy whipping cream

1. In a small bowl, mix the flour, sugar and salt; cut in the butter and shortening until crumbly. Gradually add ice water, tossing with a fork until dough holds together when pressed. Divide dough in half. Shape each half into a disk; wrap. Refrigerate for 30 minutes or overnight.

2. In a small bowl, combine the currants and rum; let stand for 20 minutes.

3. Place ¾ cup cranberries and ¼ cup sugar in a food processor; pulse until the cranberries are coarsely chopped. Transfer to a large bowl. Add apples, tapioca, lemon juice, lemon zest, cinnamon, remaining ½ cup sugar and the currant mixture; toss to combine. Let stand for 15 minutes. Preheat oven to 400°.

4. On a lightly floured surface, roll half of dough to a ⅛-in.-thick circle; transfer to 9-in. deep-dish pie plate. Trim crust to ½ in. beyond rim of plate. Add filling.

5. Roll remaining dough to a ⅛-in.-thick circle; cut into ½-in.-wide strips. Arrange over filling in a lattice pattern. Trim and seal strips to edge of bottom crust; if desired, flute edge. Place remaining cranberries in spaces between the lattice strips.

6. For the egg wash, in a small bowl, mix sugar and cinnamon; set aside. In another bowl, whisk egg and milk; brush over lattice top. Sprinkle with sugar mixture.

7. Bake on a lower oven rack for 25 minutes. Reduce temperature to 325°; bake until crust is golden brown and the filling is bubbly, 40-45 minutes longer.

8. Cool pie on a wire rack for 30 minutes; serve warm.

1 PIECE 508 cal., 21g fat (9g sat. fat), 54mg chol., 235mg sod., 75g carb. (38g sugars, 4g fiber), 6g pro.

1. On a lightly floured surface, roll dough to a ⅛-in.-thick circle; transfer to a 9-in. pie plate. Trim to ½ in. beyond rim of plate; flute edge. Refrigerate 30 minutes. Preheat oven to 425°.

2. Line unpricked crust with a double thickness of foil. Fill with pie weights, dried beans or uncooked rice. Bake on a lower oven rack until edge is light golden brown, 15-20 minutes. Remove foil and weights; bake until bottom is golden brown, 3-6 minutes longer. Cool on a wire rack. Reduce oven setting to 350°.

3. In a saucepan, melt butter. Remove from heat; add flour and stir until smooth. Stir in brown sugar. Return to heat; stir in milk and salt until blended. Cook and stir over medium-high heat until mixture is thickened and bubbly. Reduce heat; cook and stir mixture 2 minutes longer. Remove from heat. Stir about 1 cup hot filling into egg yolks, then return all to pan, stirring constantly. Bring to a gentle boil; cook and stir for 2 minutes longer. Remove from heat. Gently stir in vanilla. Pour into crust.

4. For meringue, beat egg whites and cream of tartar in a small bowl on medium speed until soft peaks form. Gradually beat in sugar, about 1 Tbsp. at a time, on high until stiff glossy peaks form and the sugar is dissolved. Spread evenly over hot filling, sealing edge to crust.

5. Bake until meringue is golden brown, 12-15 minutes. Cool on a wire rack for 1 hour. Refrigerate at least 3 hours before serving. Refrigerate leftovers.

1 PIECE 487 cal., 20g fat (10g sat. fat), 116mg chol., 330mg sod., 73g carb. (56g sugars, 0 fiber), 6g pro.

BUTTERSCOTCH PIE

PREP 30 min. + chilling
BAKE 15 min. + chilling
MAKES 8 servings

    Dough for single-crust pie
6 Tbsp. butter
6 Tbsp. all-purpose flour
1½ cup packed brown sugar
2 cups whole milk
¼ tsp. salt
3 large egg yolks, room temperature, beaten
1 tsp. vanilla extract

MERINGUE
3 large egg whites, room temperature
¼ tsp. cream of tartar
½ cup sugar

TURKEY MACARONI BAKE

PREP 15 min. **BAKE** 65 min.
MAKES 6 servings

- 2 cups cubed cooked turkey
- 1½ cups uncooked elbow macaroni
- 2 cups shredded cheddar cheese, divided
- 1 can (10¾ oz.) condensed cream of chicken soup, undiluted
- 1 cup 2% milk
- 1 can (8 oz.) mushroom stems and pieces, drained
- ¼ tsp. pepper

1. Preheat oven to 350°. In a large bowl, combine turkey, macaroni, 1½ cups cheese, soup, milk, mushrooms and pepper. Pour into a greased 2-qt. baking dish.
2. Cover and bake until macaroni is tender, 60-65 minutes. Uncover; sprinkle with remaining ½ cup cheese. Bake until cheese is melted, 5-10 minutes longer.

1¼ CUPS 359 cal., 18g fat (11g sat. fat), 85mg chol., 804mg sod., 21g carb. (3g sugars, 2g fiber), 28g pro.

GOBBLER GOODIES

PREP 30 min. **COOK** 5 min. + cooling
MAKES 28 servings

- ¼ cup butter, cubed
- 4 cups miniature marshmallows
- 6 cups crisp rice cereal
- 28 chocolate sandwich cookies
- 1½ cups chocolate frosting
- 1 pkg. (11 oz.) candy corn
- 28 malted milk balls
  White candy coating, optional

1. In a large saucepan, melt butter. Add marshmallows; stir over low heat until melted. Stir in cereal. Cool for 10 minutes. With buttered hands, form cereal mixture into 1½-in. balls. Twist apart sandwich cookies; spread frosting over each cookie half.

2. Place 28 cookie halves under cereal balls to form the base for each turkey. Place 5 pieces of candy corn in a fan pattern on each remaining cookie half; press each half onto a cereal ball to form the tails. Use frosting to attach 2 pieces of remaining candy corn to each cereal ball to form turkey wings. For each head, attach a malted milk ball with frosting; cut white tip off additional candy corn and attach to head with frosting to form beak. If desired, place melted white candy coating in a piping bag fitted with a #1 round tip; pipe onto head to form eyes. Allow to stand until the frosting has set. Store, tightly covered, at room temperature.

1 PIECE 222 cal., 6g fat (2g sat. fat), 0 chol., 125mg sod., 43g carb. (31g sugars, 1g fiber), 1g pro.

Handcrafted

CREATE A FEELING OF HOME

JOT IT DOWN

WHAT YOU'LL NEED

Wooden board
2 curtain rod hooks
2 screws
Dowel
Stain
2 paint stir sticks
Butcher paper roll
Drill
Saw
Foam brush or rag
Nail gun

DIRECTIONS

1. Begin by pre-drilling holes in wooden board for the hooks. Screw hooks into place.
2. Cut a dowel down to desired length, fitting it within the width of the board.
3. Stain dowel and paint stir sticks to a color of your choice with foam brush or rag; dry thoroughly.
4. Nail each stick horizontally into place on upper and lower portions of the wooden board, nailing only 1 end of each stick.
5. Slide a butcher paper roll onto the dowel and set the dowel into place on the hooks.
6. Unroll the paper and feed it through the stir sticks, against the wooden board.

SNACK JARS

WHAT YOU'LL NEED

Mason jars, with matching lids and rings

Green, orange and white paint

Spray sealant

Wine corks

Floral picks

Paintbrushes

Fine-grit sandpaper

Hot glue gun

DIRECTIONS

1. Paint lids and rings green, and the outside of the jars orange or white. Dry thoroughly.

2. Use fine-grit sandpaper to gently distress paint.

3. Spray sealant over lids and jars, working in a well-ventilated area. Dry thoroughly.

4. Hot-glue a wine cork to the center of each lid and add pieces of floral picks around the cork.

OWL WREATH

WHAT YOU'LL NEED

Jute place mat, sized to fit inside wreath form

Grapevine wreath

Wood slices, various sizes

2 canning jar rings

2 metal washers

Small craft feather picks

Bark pieces

Hot glue gun

DIRECTIONS

1. Hot-glue jute place mat on back side of grapevine wreath.

2. Hot-glue 2 large wood slices at top of wreath for eyes. Add detail in layers by gluing on canning rings, washers and then smaller wood slices.

3. Hot-glue craft feather picks for eyebrows. Make wings by layering and gluing pieces of bark and any additional craft picks.

Winter

A group of bull elk grazing in a snow-covered mountain forest in Rocky Mountain National Park, Colorado.

The Good Life

O CHRISTMAS TREE!

This sweet tree farm's one-month sales season
is a joyful blur of activity

KELLY SWEET GREAT BARRINGTON, MA

My name is Kelly Sweet and this is my fifth Christmas season at Seekonk Tree Farm. We're located in the Berkshires of western Massachusetts, about 2½ hours north of New York City and 2½ hours west of Boston. We offer cut-your-own and pre-cut trees plus all the accouterments.

My father-in-law, Pete Sweet Sr., started the farm on a part-time basis. He is an expert cultivator and knows everything about his trees. He also worked as the industrial arts teacher at our local middle school—so he knows everyone. The farm consists of three 7-acre lots, and we mostly grow Canaan fir, Fraser fir (the two most popular varieties), concolor fir, white spruce and white pine trees.

Pete Sr. has two sons: Pete Jr. (my husband) and Chris. Chris and his family live on a 7-acre lot across the road from Pete Sr. and his wife, Carol Sweet. Pete and Carol's acreage includes the family's original (and still primary) cut-your-own field. Chris runs a successful tree-service business and his wife, Jill Sweet, is a school nurse. They sell trees on weekends to help with overflow. Pete Jr. and I live up the road and work the family's third field. Our lot is where the tall trees (9 to 12 feet) grow and is also home to a brand-new farm stand/workshop.

To say 2020 was challenging would be an understatement. My father-in-law had a hip replacement in January and finished eight weeks of radiation treatment for prostate cancer. And my lovely mother-in-law, Carol, was not able to help out like she used to. Physically and mentally, none of us entered that season at our strongest. But we had thousands of visitors in four weeks.

We took every imaginable COVID-19 precaution and spent months speculating what this season would look like. Did we have enough inventory? Would the state shut down cut-your-own operations? Would customers be afraid to visit? We took several actions to spread out the volume and help everyone feel safe. Starting in October we offered online reservations for pre-tagging taller trees. We opened an online store to sell "farmer's choice" pre-cuts, allowing contactless payment and curbside pickup.

We also opened a third field/farm stand as a retail location for our tall trees, each of which often require two or three people to process and load onto customers' cars. By selling the "talls" at just one location, we hoped to decrease labor and time at the busy cut-your-own lots and spread out the traffic and parking.

Left: Pete Jr. and Kelly work tirelessly to keep the family business growing. Above: Chris puts the mechanical shaker to work.

I expected a nice wintry scene but when I got down there, the lack of trees stunned me.

Brothers Pete Jr. and Chris prepare a large tree for a customer, giving it a fresh cut to encourage the absorption of water.

NICE WEATHER & RECORD SALES

Nov. 26 As always, Thanksgiving (Opening Day Eve) was very busy. We've had customers showing up since last weekend. Thankfully, the forecast calls for sun all weekend.

Nov. 27 Oh. My. Goodness. Chaos! Phones ringing off the hook! Cars are everywhere! Thankfully Chris opened his side today, because the main cut-your-own lot was totally overcrowded. I'll remember the look of disbelief on Pete Sr.'s face forever: He had never seen it so busy. Despite his hurting hip, he greeted as many people as he could as he handed out freshly sanitized saws. Everyone is exhausted after this record-breaking day, and we still have 28 days to go!

Nov. 28 It was 58 degrees and busier than yesterday. I'm concerned about not having enough wreaths for the week, never mind for the season.

COVID canceled my plans to hold decorating classes in the workshop, but I was able to gather my "pod" for a girls night. They were a huge help in making centerpieces and swags to supplement our inventory.

Nov. 29 More nice weather made today's high sales volume tolerable. We learned from customers that the tree farms on Cape Cod were closed due to COVID and many Boston-area farms were sold out, which explained why so many people came to us. We ran out of small wreaths, but Pete Sr. pulled in a favor from a friend to get more. Pete Jr.'s daughter Danielle volunteered to pick them up.

Nov. 30 The customers keep coming—far more than we usually see the Monday after Thanksgiving. I spent every spare moment today assuring people by phone that we have trees and will be open next weekend. Web orders are way up; people are worried we'll sell out.

Dec. 2 Though it's Wednesday, we did the same amount of business we'd see on a typical (pre-pandemic) Saturday. Many of our new customers moved to the area this year to escape cities. Seems quite a few left their tree stands behind, because we're almost out of those, too!

PRECIPITATION & WREATHS

Dec. 3 A storm is predicted for next Saturday. Some customers love to cut trees when it's snowing—and this could make for a huge weekend. Our crew must be exhausted, but they aren't showing it.

Dec. 4 The local weatherman debuted a "Tree Cutting Forecast" today, predicting that Saturday would be a lousy day for Christmas-tree hunting and advising viewers to shop for trees today or Sunday. Pete headed out to help manage today's harvest and fulfill online and pre-tagged orders; meanwhile I threw on warm clothes and had a mini freakout when I arrived at the farm stand because customers were already there. We use Square to process credit cards—this is a new feature at the farm. Square's reports show that so far this year nearly 65% of our customers are first-timers.

Dec. 5 The weather calls for rain until 1 p.m., to be followed by a nor'easter. While customers love the picturesque beauty of fresh snow, the wet, heavy stuff and strong winds create a bad scenario for the farm. Thinking ahead, Pete Sr. stored as much product as he could under tarps and tents. The snow ultimately missed us, but it was a sideways, rainy, windy, muddy mess. Shoppers still came, but at a slower pace that allowed us to prepare for tomorrow.

Pete Jr. is almost done building the new farm stand—a gorgeous space with rough-cut pine counters, large posts and beams, and beautiful shelving. We probably spent too much time decorating and adding new merchandise; we should have been making wreaths, but it was more fun bringing the shop to life.

Dec. 6 The Tree Cutting Forecast was spot on. This was our busiest day ever, but we managed it well. Cars were parking on the roads, so Pete Sr. directed traffic all day. Many customers came to the tall-tree lot requesting to cut from us instead of the cut-your-own lots. We allowed it, but in general I am against letting customers cut their own tall trees. For one thing, they're really heavy, so people can't bring them to us for processing. We also have to protect the tagged tall trees. Many people don't know that once a tall tree is cut, it'll be 12 years or more before its replacement gets as tall. It's a real loss if someone cuts the top 9 feet from a 12-foot tree and leaves the other 3 feet behind.

Dec. 7 Reviewing the weekend's aftermath, I declared the decorating department "toast" and we started making wreaths and garlands from scratch again. Since the family has been doing this for so long, we have all kinds of homemade equipment for making seasonal decor.

Trees and handmade wreaths were in major demand all season long.

Dec. 8 There's endless trimming of brush to be done to create our accessories. I love the smell of pine, but the pine pitch can be so annoying—today I felt like a bear with my mask on and my sticky "honey" hands.

Dec. 9 COVID-19 prevented us from offering some of the usual extras, like hot cocoa and cider. Last year, we sold maple cotton candy made from our own syrup, but this year that was another casualty. At one point a little boy got out of his parents' car, headed directly to the farm stand window and asked for two bags of cotton candy. His father looked at me expectantly. The boy was so sad to hear we didn't have it this year that I felt like I'd ruined his Christmas. I promised that next year he could get a free bag, which might have prevented a meltdown.

BIG DEMAND, SHRINKING SUPPLY
Dec. 10 Pete Sr. has started taking pain medication for his hip—albeit reluctantly—and he managed to do his rounds to get an inventory for the coming weekend.

Dec. 12 We usually have lots of time to prepare for crowded days. But we've sold nearly a season's worth of trees in three weeks, so everything is a rush. Tasks that used to be done once a week—like cutting rope into sections to tie trees onto cars—are daily jobs now. We keep making new wreaths, and they sell right away. Today was solidly busy. At dinner, Pete Sr. said he thought at least some aspect of the farm could stay open until Christmas Eve.

Dec. 13 Another snowstorm is forecast, plus word has gotten out that we may close soon, so the pace is frantic. The Sweet men dumped wood chips on our parking areas and paths to keep people from sinking into the mud. As I drove up the hill to drop off wreaths, I saw that lots 2 and 3 looked decimated; the most popular trees (between 7 and 8 feet tall) were in very low supply. Some customers came back from the cut-your-own fields saying they couldn't find a tree in the height they wanted. They had to select from our pre-cuts. Others opted to buy a tall tree and have us cut it to a shorter height.

Pete Jr. talked to his dad about closing the main field and moving all the pre-cuts to the farm stand so we could keep at least one location open. Closing the main lot

isn't ideal, but it seems like the only option—even though there are regular customers who haven't made it out yet, along with people who need their trees as fresh as possible because they decorate with real candles. But we are all agreed that we can keep the farm stand lot open.

Dec. 14 We turned Pete Sr. and Carol's sales area back into a normal backyard while a few lucky folks got to cut the last trees there. We removed the tree racks and moved the remaining inventory to our lot, and Pete Sr. made signs for the end of his driveway indicating that his lot was closed for the season.

Dec. 15 I can't believe Christmas is still 10 days away! My husband keeps finding trees to cut down in our picked-over lots. I told him it's a good thing I'm not a tree or he might cut me down, too!

Dec. 16 The storm today turned out to be a big deal, but much of the extra work that comes with a storm wasn't a factor this year, since our pick-your-own operation was closed for the season. In the past, we've had to dig trees out and blow them off, plus make paths so folks could access them. It's a ton of work, and none of us are sad about missing out on it.

FORCED TO CLOSE EARLY

Dec. 17 It's a blizzard! The farm is closed. We appreciate the break, although the phone keeps ringing with people still asking if they can come cut a tree today.

Dec. 18 This morning I ran down to our lot to take a picture. I expected a nice wintry scene, but the lack of trees stunned me. These trees only grow 1 foot per year, and I'm afraid we're cannibalizing next year's stock.

Dec. 19 Chris and Pete Sr. went hunting for more pre-cuts first thing today. But harvesting trees in 16 inches of snow is no fun. Given that we've all made our money for the year, I know they're doing the extra work out of the goodness of their hearts.

I heard on NPR that real trees are commanding $2,500 each in Manhattan! Between the media frenzy, the emotions tied up in honoring or starting traditions during a pandemic, and the high prices in New York, I'm afraid we'll have more customers than resources allow. (I'd drive a six-hour round trip to save $2,400—wouldn't you?)

The phone started ringing early. All calls were from NYC metro area codes, and the callers expressed degrees of

The 2020 tree season was one for the record books, and the Sweets had to end their season early to save stock for 2021.

desperation. I cautioned that we were first-come, first-served business and had a limited supply.

Things got a little bumpy. A few customers looked at our available selection and left. Others wanted to buy $150 trees for $65 because they only needed the top 6 to 7 feet. Most amazingly, one guy went into our field with his own saw and helped himself to a tagged 7-footer!

Dec. 20 The short trees got their day in the sun today because they're pretty much all we have left.

Dec. 21 Our lot had 10 remaining trees, so Pete Jr. opened the farm stand with Danielle. He's distressed by our decision to stop cutting, but he knows it's the right thing to do to ensure we have trees for next year.

Dec. 22 Sold out by noon and closed for the season. We updated our voicemail and websites and did some organizing for next year. Pete Jr. called someone who'd arranged to pick up a tree on Christmas Eve; they changed the date to tomorrow

so we can block the driveway after that. If we're seen down there on Christmas Eve, people will think we're open. I tease Pete about hiding, but that's exactly what we need to do.

Dec. 23 A woman called to say her tree was fully decorated but the stand had sprung a leak. I knew we had one left at the shop but told her we were closed for the season. She sounded distraught, so I said to call back if she couldn't find anything else. A few hours later, the woman's mother called. I offered to meet them nearby. When we met up, they gave me a delicious box of cookies, like a nice scene from a Hallmark movie.

Dec. 24 We typically sell anywhere from 10 to 25 trees on Christmas Eve, so Pete Jr. is worried that people will be upset the farm is closed. Still, we had a nice dinner with Carol and Pete Sr., exchanged gifts and starting planning for 2021.

Dec. 25 Yes, someone did call asking if they could cut a tree today. And yes, I answered the phone. Merry Christmas!

ONE IN A MILLION

Teacher Jennifer Williams is on a quest to give away books—lots and lots of books!

BY JILL GLEESON APPALACHIAN MOUNTAINS, PA

Ask Jennifer Williams if she has any children, and she'll reply, "Just the thousands I've had over 33 years of teaching." The Danville, Virginia, resident is so dedicated to her kids that she converted the guest room in the house she shares with her husband, Scott Williams, into a classroom for extracurricular tutoring. And then there are her book giveaways, which she hopes will eventually total a million volumes.

Jennifer says her project began with an observation. She noticed how often kids would ask to keep the books she read with them because they didn't have access to books at home.

"There's no denying that you can tell kids who are exposed to books, or have books, by the vocabulary they use, the way they carry themselves, or how they answer questions or retell a simple story," Jennifer says. "All these things improve with reading. And so it became my mission to give away as many books as I could."

As for the specific number, Jennifer says she wanted "to do something big."

To that end, Jennifer gives away books at grade schools in and around Danville—including her own, Chatham Elementary School. She also founded a book group in the Danville County Jail, where the participants get to keep what they read. On top of that, she stocks more than 40 Little Free Libraries and hosts summer reading camps—with book giveaways—for disadvantaged city youth.

Since she began formally giving books away in the spring of 2017, Jennifer has handed out more than a 100,000 volumes.

And she figures she's spent more than $25,000 of her own money doing so, though she also accepts books and monetary donations.

Jennifer, who says that she inherited her bookworm ways from her librarian mother, loves "the magic that happens when a kid discovers a story they truly love and then they get to own it and read it again and again."

"Or they find a book that looks like one that they'll love," she says. "And the same smile spreads over their face. I love what I do."

Jennifer Williams regularly stocks more than 40 Little Free Libraries with books.

FARMING IN A PRAIRIE PROVINCE

Two Montana State alumni raise livestock, crops and
a happy family in Western Canada

JILL BURKHARDT GWYNNE AB, CANADA

Hello! My name is Jill Burkhardt. I grew up on a row-crop and hog farm in east-central Illinois, then my parents moved us to Montana to raise cattle. I attended university in Bozeman, which is where I met my husband, Kelly Burkhardt. We each have a degree in range science. I started my career working for the U.S. Bureau of Land Management, and in Canada for the Alberta provincial government.

Kelly and I, along with our kids, are the fourth and fifth generations of Burkhardts to own Crooked Lake Farm near Gwynne, Alberta, Canada. Kelly's family came here by train from North Dakota in 1900, and his great-grandfather Otto Burkhardt purchased our home-quarter in 1918. The original homestead is a quarter mile north of our house. Kelly and I moved to the farm in 2004 but worked off-farm until 2010, when we took over management of the farm from his dad, Gary Burkhardt, who still helps with it today.

Our farm is considered a mixed farm because we raise both livestock and crops. We have 150 cows and 110 calves (steers and heifers) in our backgrounding feedlot. In spring we seed a combined 1,000 acres of canola, oats, malt barley and wheat. We grow all the feed for our cattle and bale about 1,000 round bales on 450 acres. The cattle are pastured in summer on 850 acres of deeded and rented land.

We focus on low-stress handling and do much of our work on foot, using horses or quads to move cattle home in the fall. Our pastures are rotationally grazed. In the summer, the cattle know that when they see a person, fresh grass awaits!

Afternoon found us doing chores in a balmy 3 degrees Fahrenheit.

In 2012, we started finishing a few steers and marketing our beef direct to consumers. We began by going to Edmonton farmers markets, but now we sell wholesale to a deli there, and by word of mouth. Our cattle are not given artificial hormones, and we give them antibiotics only when medically necessary. We participate in the Canadian Verified Beef Plus program, and we follow a rigorous vaccination program, working closely with our vet if issues occur. If an animal requires antibiotics, that animal is treated and removed from the direct beef program.

All of our kids are home-schooled. Our son CJ is in grade 11, daughter, Brynn, is in grade 4 and son Blayne is in kindergarten. In my spare time, I'm a freelance writer for a provincial agriculture newspaper.

Left: Born to farmers in east-central Illinois, Jill Burkhardt now calls Canada home. Above: Blayne helps tend to the chickens.

DOING CHORES, FAMILY-STYLE

Jan. 1 Although our province is in temporary lockdown due to the pandemic, I'm excited for a new year. January is typically slow, but there are still the day-to-day chores, plus whatever activity life with livestock brings. Today Brynn, Blayne and I went snowshoeing to check the fence around the grazing corn, and the kids tried to identify tracks in the snow. We found that the mice enjoy our corn, and the coyotes and foxes have been busy chasing mice!

Jan. 2 On this beautiful day we decided to get the cornfield ready for grazing. Last year we put in 10 acres so we'd be able to get away for a week without worrying about feeding the herd. We upped it to 20 acres this year and had good heat and moisture, so things really grew!

We used a skid-steer and bucket to flatten out where the cross fencing was going to go. Then Brynn and I pounded in rebar posts. Brynn drove the side-by-side while I measured out where the posts would go. We had five paddocks and hoped to get six to eight weeks of grazing out of the field. Brynn also helped me feed the bulls, do chicken chores and prep for butchering roosters. We keep around 40 heritage-breed hens for eggs and have a few roosters so we can grow our own replacements.

Kelly operates a drill press in the workshop.

CJ fed the cows and loaded the TMR mixer (a wagon in which hay, haylage and other feed are mixed) so Kelly could fill the feedlot bunks. We mix roughly 4,500 pounds of feed for the 110 weaned feedlot calves. The filled bunks last two to three days, depending on weather. The calves eat more when it's colder. To help prevent waste, we rake up the feed for the calves every day.

Jan. 3 Brynn, CJ and I caught roosters and set up to butcher. Our neighbor helped and the job went fast. We were even able to use the old plucker that Kelly's grandfather Richard Burkhardt made more than 40 years ago. Later CJ helped me cut up the chicken. He is a hands-on learner and caught on fast.

Jan. 4 Today was the kids' first day back at school after Christmas break. While the older two were learning online, I worked with Blayne on his letters and numbers. There are no online lessons on Fridays, which gives us an open day for homework, farm chores or whatever needs to be finished.

Jan. 5 Brynn and Blayne rode along in the tractor while I fed cows. The kids like to open gates and pull the netwrap off bales. We fed hay with a shredder and put oat straw in bunk feeders. CJ helped Gary in the shop and fed the horses and his 4-H steer. Meanwhile, Brynn collected eggs and helped me feed the chickens and grain the bulls.

Jan. 6 Today was a big chore day. We also needed to prepare a report on our inventory for the bank. So while Kelly and I waited for the mixer to ready feed for the feedlot, we counted bales.

Jan. 7 We want our cattle to have the best nutrition, so we make sure they get the right minerals and vitamins. After Gary got home from picking up mineral, he went out with the skid-steer to clear willows from the crop fields. We've had wet weather the past two years, so willow and poplar saplings grew in areas we couldn't crop. Trees grow fast in our area, so we try to control them when they're small.

COWS IN THE CORN

Jan. 8 Kelly hauled his last load of wheat today. He shoveled and cleaned out three bins as he loaded, which took the better

CJ plays a big hand on the farm and pitches in on neighbors' farms too.

part of the day. Brynn and Blayne played in the shop while I fixed fence-wire reels. We use temporary fencing around the farmyard in spring and summer to graze the yard and the area around buildings instead of mowing.

Jan. 9 I headed to Camrose to pick up our weekly Loop load at the local grocery. Today's haul was relatively small. After sorting, we had six boxes of produce for the feedlot calves; greens, raspberries and sandwiches for the chickens; and fried chicken for the cats. We donated half a box of meat, two big bags of Christmas goodies and a box of baked goods to people in need.

Jan. 10 Putting in the rest of the cross fencing took much longer than I expected. One reel wasn't wound correctly last summer, so when I unrolled the wire, it came off in knots and wrapped around the reel. My attempts to fix it in the field were thwarted, so I grabbed the other reel and unwound it to find that I was 25 yards short. I went to the shop to find more wire, untangled it, finished the cross fence and finally let the cows in for corn grazing. They happily ran in and started eating.

Jan. 11 In a virtual meeting with the research committee for Alberta Beef Producers, we discussed ranking and funding research proposals. CJ raked feed for the weaned calves and fed his steer and the horses. Brynn and Blayne did chicken chores and made sure the cows were in the correct paddock. The kids did great!

Jan. 12 I spoke with our cattle marketer after lunch. He helps us find markets for our feeder steers, heifers and cull cows, and sends out weekly market reports. He asked when we want to sell specific groups of animals in order to find buyers in advance. It's a new concept for us, and I hope it works!

Some customers stopped by for straw bales. We bought a used baler about five years ago because it was hard to find small square bales in our area. We put up about 200 hay and 100 straw bales this year for our use and to sell. As we drove to check on the cows in the corn, Gary came out and said he thought they were farther south than they should be. Sure enough, they were in the next paddock. (I was shocked—150 cows ate around 4 acres of corn in a day and a half!) I quickly put up the wire between paddocks 5 and 6 to stop them and phoned CJ to come help. Gary, Brynn and Blayne rolled up fence between paddocks 3 and 4 and found that one of the insulators had slid down the rebar post, enabling the cows to walk over

Red tags along on chores, ready to jump in as needed.

cow-chasing day. Today's hero was our heeler, Red, who got the cows to move into the correct paddock.

Jan. 18 Since we don't have a barn to shelter our cows, I found them gathered around their bed pack (a large area of straw bedding) behind the windbreaks. The wind was howling again; the rain had stopped, but snow had fallen overnight. Brynn and Blayne made slides out of the drifts that formed between rows of bales. Kelly had 600 pounds of hay left after filling the bunks, so he gave it to the cows for a treat. I said he's going to spoil them!

Jan. 20 Yesterday's visibility was less than 10 yards. Today the wind continued, but the sun shone and the temperature wasn't bad. Still, 32 degrees Fahrenheit has a bite when combined with 25 mph winds, so we minimized our time outside. Kelly worked in the shop installing a new LED light bar on a tractor. This time of year, we get only about eight hours of light a day, so good lighting is important!

We ate home-raised steaks and potatoes from our garden for supper. I freeze, can, pickle and preserve all that our garden produces, because (among other reasons) I love eating the bounty in the middle of winter. It gives me great hope that spring and summer will eventually come!

Jan. 21 Kelly and Gary decided to grind chop. We have a small 200-bushel bin for storing ground oats and fava beans. We use this to give the feedlot calves and bulls about 4 pounds of grain per head per day to help meet their nutritional needs.

SUBZERO TEMPS & CATTLE SHENANIGANS

Jan. 22 Kelly opened the feedlot gate to the alleyway and three calves rushed out. They eventually turned around, and one heifer ran under a low board and into the bull pen. CJ and Brynn helped me get her back where she belonged.

Jan. 23 I went outside and the wind and cold smacked me in the face! It was -1 degree Fahrenheit, and the wind chill was -20. Winter has returned. Brynn and I checked the solar fences to make sure the panels were clear.

Jan. 24 When it's this cold out, chores seem endless. We warmed up with a hot supper of chicken, potatoes, green beans and Saskatoon berry crisp with whipped

the electric fence. CJ and I walked the cows back to paddock 4 and held them there while Gary rolled wire for the temporary fence.

Jan. 13 The kids did school, and Kelly called the agronomist to plan spring crops. He spent the better part of the day figuring out rotations and researching new varieties. He also filed his crop plan with the agronomy company so we can get fertilizer rates for the spring. They have our soil-sample information; now they can configure blends specifically for each field. He'll give the plan to our crop-insurance carrier to get a quote for the coming year.

CHASING COWS & GRINDING CHOP

Jan. 15 The cows were out again! The cross fence to the south was down and they were in the next paddock. We think a moose walked through the fence— they're strong enough to pull the wire until it breaks, often pulling out fence staples or even posts as they go.

Jan. 16 Brynn and Blayne joined me for Loop pickup. On our way to town, we took our garbage to the transfer station since we don't have on-farm pickup. The station is only open twice a week. While I sorted Loop, Kelly fed calves and the kids amused themselves by pulling one another in a sled behind the ATV.

Jan. 17 What began as a simple "unhook the wire and put it back in the insulator" turned into another

cream—another meal that we raised and foraged ourselves. Saskatoon berries are native and grow on bushes in our pastures in the summer. The kids love eating them while we pick!

Jan. 25 Surprisingly, some of the cows are still grazing on corn in this weather. Others are hunkered down on the cozy straw bed pack surrounded by windbreaks. I went to see how the calves were faring. I can't believe how fat and roly-poly some of them are! While in the pen, I noticed ice around the waterer. Sure enough, the float was stuck. Kelly helped me chip the ice away. When we took off the cover, we saw that a wing nut had come loose, so we tightened it up and put the float back in place. Working in water in this weather is no fun! My gloves froze in seconds.

Jan. 26 Kelly chopped wood for the stove, which we run when temps dip below 14 degrees Fahrenheit. When our furnace has a hard time keeping up, the stove makes the house warm and toasty.

Jan. 27 The cows went a few days without misbehaving, but they broke their streak this morning by knocking down the wire to the next paddock. Kelly went out to see if he could get them back. He took the dogs with him, and though they are very handy, he still needed my help.

Jan. 28 We got a few inches of snow overnight, so CJ went to the neighbor's to shovel. After bringing him home, I saw five heifers in the next paddock again. Four sneaked under the electric wire and one jumped over it! Thankfully they all came running for hay.

Jan. 29 Kelly met with our agronomy company to go over software. After doing online meetings for so long, it felt strange having someone in our home again!

I filled out data on our weaned calves and determined pregnancy-checking statistics. Our farm is part of a four-year Canada-wide cow-calf surveillance project that is gathering info about diseases and other issues important to the industry.

Afternoon found us doing chores in a balmy 3 degrees Fahrenheit. Kelly fed leftover feed to the bulls, who were out of hay, and I used the skid-steer to pry some bottom bales from our square-bale stack and then took them to the horses.

Jan. 31 Kelly, Brynn, Blayne and I set up to weigh the calves. Kelly made sure all the gates around the chute could open. We also chipped ice around the scale, set it in place (we weigh our calves in the alleyway of the handling system) and then put the calves in the holding pen. Red helped, zigzagging behind the calves to group them and then moving them as one unit.

Weighing the calves did not go smoothly. For one thing, they didn't want to step onto the scale, which was icy from being housed outside. We weighed 83 of the 111 calves, then called it a day since it was getting dark and the calves were uncooperative. We fed the bulls and put parasiticide on them; a few were so itchy from lice they were rubbing on fence posts to scratch themselves. We fed the horses, CJ fed his steer, Brynn helped me check the chickens and we came in for the night.

I hope you've enjoyed following along with daily life on our farm. Although January is typically a slow month for us, there are always a few unexpected events that keep us on our toes and ever busy!

Snow-capped bales make a good place for children to play.

Scrapbook

CAPTURE THE BEAUTY AROUND YOU

1. HOME, SWEET HOME

As soon as I hung this edible birdhouse, I noticed my resident bluebird pair inspecting it, despite already having four nest boxes! They seem to be in deep discussion over whether to love it or list it.

GRETCHEN DUNHAM FRANKLIN, TN

2. WHAT ABOUT THAT ONE?

One of the most fun and relaxing events leading up to Christmas is when we visit a local tree farm to pick out the perfect tree. Family moments like this create the best memories.

CAROLYN ANDERSON NEW ALEXANDRIA, PA

1

1. BIRDS OF A FEATHER

My daughter Lilly is only 4 years old, but she's already set up a business selling eggs from our farm. She calls it Lilly's Layin Ladies, and with some help from the rest of the family, she does everything it takes to keep her business running.

SHAYLYN JOHNSON LAKETOWN, UT

2. WINTER WILDLIFE

It was mesmerizing to watch these bison using their heads to search for grass against the background of Wyoming's Teton Mountains.

SHARON PLOWMAN HARRISONBURG, VA

3. COLD SUPPER

It was a very cold winter day at only 3 degrees when I took this photo in northern New Hampshire, within a mile of the Canadian border. The robin seemed to be very happy while feasting on the abundance of mountain ash berries.

PAUL BLOSSOM BRAINTREE, VT

1. FREEZE FRAME

This moose was just minding her own business on a very chilly morning.

HEIDI MASON DOUGLAS, WY

2. NEW ADVENTURES

On our first vacation to Colorado's beautiful mountains, we took a snowmobiling trip and snapped a family photo at Alpine Lake.

REAGAN McKINLEY BRYANT, AR

3. DAY IS DONE

Resting in Dam Lake's serene glow was the perfect end to a fun day in northern Wisconsin.

TAMRIN NAVARRO WHEATON, IL

3

FORM A LINE
Last year was one of the coldest
winters we'd experienced recently,
and we were more or less shut
in because of heavy snow cover.
I walked outside one day and saw
these birds sitting pretty on an old
clothesline post—from left to right,
a male and female northern cardinal,
a purple finch and a dark-eyed junco.

KAY CRAIG SPURLOCK WILMAR, AR

1

1. HIGH FLYING
For a few glorious seconds, this boy's sled flew into the air, making him king of the mountain.

JOHN NEFF FLETCHER, NC

2. CHRISTMAS VACATION
Our warm-weather families from Arizona and Kauai traveled to Mount Charleston, Nevada, for the holidays. It was so cold up in the snow!

SHARON PRICE MESA, AZ

3. A WARM HELLO ON A CHILLY DAY
Our grandson Bodie wandered over to chat with our miniature donkey, Buck, during a snowstorm.

KAREN & MARK STEINER ORRVILLE, OH

1. ON THE MOVE

We have deep snowfalls here in the Cascade Range, and our birds have to be creative to remain healthy and fed. A large blue spruce tree provides wonderful cover, and I scatter seeds on the branches. This offers me an optimal area to study bird behaviors—and to take photos. I call this image "The March of the California Quails."

DOUGLAS BEALL CAMP SHERMAN, OR

2. PET PROJECT

On our family farm, chore time often turns into playtime, especially for these two mischievous boys. Owen, 8, loves visiting his goat, Teeter.

ECHOE DAVIS FAIRBURY, NE

3. HAYING HELP

My husband and I live on a cattle ranch and dryland wheat farm. My sister-in-law, Anna McCorkle, took this sweet photo of our daughter "working" with her dad.

JESSICA HOARD DAVENPORT, WA

1. SNACK TIME

Before a rare winter storm in Mississippi, I made this DIY feeder and filled it with homemade suet. Birds flocked to it, often fighting for a spot to sit and eat. The white-throated sparrow seems to be saying "Is there room for me?" as it flies in to find an empty perch. The cardinals, sparrows, juncos, pine warblers and house finches kept me busy filling the feeder multiple times each day.

PENNY RICE OAKLAND, MS

2. TREAD CAREFULLY

I was lucky to be biking in Sedona, Arizona, when it snowed. The contrast between the white powder and red rock was stunning.

GRANT CLOUD WHITELAND, IN

3. THE BEST GIFT OF ALL

Instead of exchanging Christmas presents, we gifted each other a trip to Rocky Mountain National Park.

BRITTANY TATYREK HITCHCOCK, TX

1. WE CAN DO IT!

Every year we cut our own Christmas tree at a nearby farm. This time we got a second one for the kids. We loved seeing them work together, determined to haul their tree up the hill on their own.

CYNTHIA SCHARENBROCH MARSHFIELD, WI

2. SWEET DREAMS

Playing outside can be exhausting! Lucy fell asleep on her sled ride!

KRISTI ANDERSON HARTFORD, SD

3. SNOWY SURPRISE

My daughter smashed a snowball in her brother's face just before I snapped this photo. He was a bit shocked, as this was his first snow, but he took it like a champ.

SHAYE COBB BLAIRSVILLE, GA

Heart & Soul

ROAD TO HEALING

A solitary journey on the open highway helps
a granddaughter work through life and loss

GRACE HANSEN REXBURG, ID

On the morning two days after Christmas 2020, I crept out of my motel room in Hurricane, Utah. The journey—a solo road trip from my home in Idaho Falls, Idaho, to two Arizona national parks—was an attempt at coming to terms with my grandmother's terminal cancer diagnosis.

She was 90 years old, and the doctors didn't mince words—she had two to three months left to live without intervention. Six months after her diagnosis and eight weeks prior to Christmas, she'd started going blind. With each day, her eyesight faded. So, it also seemed, did her will to continue fighting what she knew would ultimately be a losing battle.

As I passed Utah's southern border into Arizona's northern desert, I tried to stop thinking about death and started calculating mileage. To arrive at Petrified Forest National Park by early afternoon, I would have to drive the vast adjoining Navajo reservation in five hours. If I hurried, I could spend a few hours in the park before making my way to Flagstaff and on to Tucson. All of that meant at least an 11-hour day in the car.

I shifted against my leather seat and took a sip of caffeinated water as the scenery drifted into focus. Reddish plateaus stacked on the horizon, their rocky outlines stenciled neatly in every direction. The sky startled awake, pinks and oranges spreading up into the darkness, shifting in stages into blue. I grasped the wheel harder, struck by the enormity.

The stark comparison between my insignificance and the vastness of the desert overwhelmed me. I had left my home, cozy with blankets and family and cheer, for this very reason. After a few seconds, the spectacular scenery short-circuited my capacity to absorb it. I could not understand the landscape any better than I could understand death. I drove straight into the sunrise.

ROAD TO DISCOVERY

That afternoon in Petrified Forest National Park, I wandered over shallow hills under an overcast sky. I squatted next to the petrified remains of a massive log. At some point in its millions of years of history, it had broken into perfectly sliced sections, as if an ambitious lumberjack had sawed it apart.

I touched the cold shell of what once had been bark, and then I spread my hand out across the weathered surface. My grandma had never been to that part of the state. Now, she never would go.

My legs, stiff from driving for so many hours, protested as I stood and stretched. I wanted to stay and explore the haunting, beautiful landscape longer. But there was more to see and many miles to drive, so I

regretfully slid back into my car and eased away.

A word nagged at my thoughts as I left the park and cruised toward Flagstaff: *privilege*. It had been a privilege to see those trees, older than any of us would ever be. But, as was true of so many things in my life, the whole experience was possible because of privilege. As a former lawyer and current teacher, I have financial and scheduling flexibility that many people don't. I chose to leave a happy, holiday-sated family behind for a few days of adventure and self-discovery on my own because it felt necessary.

By the time I reached Flagstaff, the sun had long set, and I turned south in darkness and silence. I pushed up and down the mountain passes toward Phoenix. I had seen a place my grandmother never would. It was a privilege, all of it, and I was determined

Grace marvels at ancient logs in Petrified Forest National Park (above) and found solace in the arid landscapes of the Southwest (opposite).

Saguaro cactuses tower over the underbrush in Saguaro National Park.

true as I traced a finger up the cool, smooth valley between two ridges of spines—then my own life and death, and those of my grandmother, must as well. That knowledge did not ease the grief and the uncertainty of life's inevitable end. It did validate it though, somehow.

FOREVER FAMILY

Hours later, pulling into my aunt's Las Vegas driveway in the dark, I felt myself relax into the warm comfort of her presence. We'd lived 10 hours apart my entire life, but when she looked at me, it was my grandmother's soft blue eyes that I saw. We hugged and smiled, exchanging stories from our months of absence. Eventually, we talked about the woman who linked us more closely than geography or age ever could.

My aunt is 70 years old, more than 40 years my senior and my grandmother's firstborn. As we sat in her kitchen, she asked me to tell her about her mother.

Again, the word *privilege* drifted into my mind. My house was only a few minutes from my grandma's. I saw her several times a week, sometimes every day. It's been agonizing to watch her futilely fight cancer and aging, but I'm honored to witness the final stages of a life that began all the way back in 1929. That life was one my aunt watched for 20 years in close, vivid detail—one I have watched for the last 20.

The next morning, as I began my final stretch toward home, my aunt left me with a snack pack and a short note. Her handwriting was nearly a replica of my grandmother's. I traveled north, and snow began to crest the mountains as they shifted from red to brown.

The sun set as I crossed into Idaho, marking four states in four days. I thought about Arizona's rocky plateaus that had revealed themselves before the sun. I wondered if, in the end, that was what death is—a darkening of the hills and a lightening of the sky.

I caught a glimpse of my eyes in the rearview mirror, the same soft blue as my aunt's and grandma's. I knew that somehow all I had seen on my journey through the Southwest, and all of the things they had seen in their lives, we had seen together.

to make it mean something. But first I had to get to Tucson.

LIVING LEGACY

The next day, I chose to explore the west side of Saguaro National Park first, mostly because I'd read that it hosted the majority of the cactuses. I was amazed by the size and number of these sentinels of the desert. They towered above the sandy, rocky ground, their arms twisting across each other and up toward the brilliant blue sky. According to the pamphlet I'd picked up at the visitor center, only a cactus that was at least 50 to 75 years old sprouted arms.

I considered that as I plodded through acre after acre of them, growing steadily more aware that I was in a forest of ancient beings. As opposed to the graveyard of the petrified trees, though, these elder statesmen were very much alive.

Saguaro cactuses thrive in the Sonoran Desert, on hillsides, in people's fenced-off yards and along the highway meridian. But mostly they are in this park.

These gnarled, green botanical anomalies (like bizarre spindly trees) made me appreciate the individual value of each of their strange, noble frames. If they were important, we must be important, too, somehow. If their lives and deaths mattered—which I could not doubt was

WINTER'S MIRACLE

A dark, cold night opens the heart to appreciate
simplicity—and embrace serenity

MAGGIE BRIGHT MONROE, WA

It's a cold December night. The land around me is blanketed with frost, and the stars above shine brighter than a thousand diamonds. The frozen earth crunches under my boots as I walk across the field to take care of the animals. The icy blades of grass glisten in the silver light of the moon like jewels in a sea.

I shiver against the chill in the air and watch as wisps of my breath float away into the darkness. The air is still and silent, and it feels as if the whole world is at peace. There are no distractions. It's nothing but me and God's creation. In this night is an all-encompassing holiness.

This is winter's miracle. Just as a flowing creek freezes over, winter has a way of halting time. And just as the aroma of Mama's cooking pulls you in, winter does, too.

I flip the light switch in the barn and am greeted by a chorus of cats' meows. I realize: Winter is light. It's the glow of the headlights of Daddy's truck pulling into the driveway. It's tree lights dancing on red ornaments. It's the Light of the World, born in a stable on a night quite like this.

I step back outside with hay in hand and close the barn door. As I walk across the field, silence once again is my only company. Winter is peace on earth. It's the holiness of a silent night, the melody of a choir singing in a snow-covered church on Sunday, the gratefulness of a family saying grace before Christmas dinner.

To me, winter is not about glitter and gifts. The greatest celebration of the season is simplicity: finding beauty in a stark landscape and a clear sky or seeing the colors of a field hushed in morning fog.

I sit down to milk the cows and revel in the sweet aroma rising from the pail in curls of steam. I breathe deeply. Maybe even this moment is worth celebrating. I celebrate my cozy evenings milking to the rhythms of songs on the radio and the cows chewing their cud. I celebrate winter every time I inhale the clean, cold air. I celebrate by baking gingerbread cookies for my family in our cozy, warm kitchen.

Once the milking is finished, all the barns are cleaned, and each animal is safe, warm and fed for the night, I walk toward the house. I slow down as I near the door. Tonight I take an extra moment to pause and look up at the stars. I think of the keeper of these stars and thank him for this night divine.

Maggie Bright lives near the mountains in idyllic Monroe, Washington.

HARD-WON WISDOM

An unruly cow and unseasonable weather
tested this young farmer

BILL WARE OKLAHOMA CITY, OK

Where I'm from in Oklahoma, winters are cold, but they usually don't include long periods of ice and snow. But the winter of 1960 was anything but normal, and there was a Sunday morning that a 14-year-old cowboy would never forget.

A big rock fireplace, the only source of heat at my end of the house, was a faint glow when the 6 o'clock alarm went off. The windows were iced over inside and out. I could see my breath.

Dad was away again so I had to feed the animals. The horses were secure in the barn, and the chickens were safe in the henhouse. What I dreaded most on this blizzardy day was milking the cow.

She produced at least 2½ gallons of milk a day, which meant a lot of time milking, pouring the milk through a separator, washing and sanitizing the bottles, and then filling them. The cow, a Guernsey, had become unpredictable and mean after the birth of her calf that fall.

I got dressed in my cold room, pulled on my cap, scarf and gloves, zipped up my jacket and stepped outside. Still, I was not adequately prepared for this day. The forecast called for 3 to 4 inches of snow but we'd gotten twice that, with winds of 10 to 20 mph. The thermometer read zero.

I trudged through the waist-high drifts toward the cow barn. As usual, the side door was open so the cows could go in and out. I tried to hop the fence and fell headfirst into the snow. I struggled to get back on top of the deep snow, gasping for air as I got to my feet. My outer pair of jeans was frozen stiff, my corduroys and long johns were cold but mostly dry, but my feet were freezing.

I stepped inside the cow barn. It was cold, dark and uncharacteristically quiet. I hit the light switch. Nothing. Back outside, I could see a trail of shadows through the blowing snow. I stepped over the fence rail and saw two sets of tracks leading off to an unknown location. My heart sank and tears froze on my face. What was I supposed to do? Dad was away on a trip. My mother and sisters were in the house, but they didn't even know I was out here. The tracks led back toward the house and veered down a ravine some 40 feet below. The only place the cow might be able to cross the creek was a high-water spillway at the far corner of the property.

I went back to my room and put on dry clothes and more socks. It was still early and no one else was stirring, but daylight had broken by the time I resumed my search for the Guernsey and her calf. The snow had stopped and the wind had calmed some, but it was still bitterly cold. I picked up a tree limb for a walking stick.

Where was that cow? I walked along the ridge behind the house, looking down across the pasture as it gradually sloped to the creek and the southeast bridge crossing. In the open 40-acre pasture,

The only place the cow might be able to cross the creek was a high-water spillway at the far corner of the property.

the wind had blown snow off the main trail and onto the grass. The cow's path was clear. I knew where she was going.

I came off the top of the ridge, stumbling and falling but determined. The bridge was covered in ice and snow, but I slid across and then doubled back toward a stand of cottonwoods on the fence line.

There she was, standing over her calf in the deep shelter of the woods, the same place Dad and I had found her and her newborn only a few months earlier. As I walked toward her, she lowered her head as a warning—apparently preparing for a standoff. Instinctively I charged, swinging my walking stick and yelling as loud as I could, "Go to the barn!"

The Guernsey gave a snort but began to move back along the path she had set, her calf at her side. She made her way across the bridge and then bolted uphill to the barn. The 1-mile journey took 30 minutes. I put feed and water in their buckets, closed the barn door and continued my early morning routine, although it was almost noon. I turned on the heater in the milk room, set up the separator, grabbed my bucket and got to work.

The Guernsey stood quietly throughout milking and, due to the late hour, she nearly filled the bucket. Finished at last!

Slowly she raised her right hind leg and placed her nasty foot in the bucket, then just as casually lifted it out. I slung that bucket with all the strength a defeated 14-year-old could muster. It bounced off the wall of the barn, showering warm milk in all directions. In my frustration I'd just added another chore to my list.

The day was difficult, to be sure. But it taught me the importance of harnessing all the experience and skills you possess to accomplish a job that has to be done, knowing that the outcome of your task may not be quite what you set out to accomplish. Despite the lack of fresh milk that morning, I was happy to return to the warmth of hearth, home and family.

Taste of the Country

BUTTERY CRESCENT ROLLS

PREP 35 min. + rising **BAKE** 10 min.
MAKES 2 dozen

- 1 Tbsp. active dry yeast
- 1 tsp. plus ⅓ cup sugar
- ½ cup warm water (110° to 115°)
- ½ cup butter, softened
- ½ cup warm 2% milk (110° to 115°)
- 1 large egg, room temperature
- ¾ tsp. salt
- 4 cups all-purpose flour

1. In a large bowl, dissolve yeast and 1 tsp. sugar in warm water. Add butter, milk, egg and salt. Add remaining ⅓ cup sugar and 2 cups flour. Beat mixture until smooth. Stir in enough remaining flour to form a soft dough.
2. Turn onto a floured surface; knead until smooth and elastic, 6-8 minutes. Place in greased bowl, turning once to grease top. Cover and let rise in a warm place until doubled, about 1 hour.
3. Punch dough down. Turn onto a lightly floured surface; divide in half. Roll each portion into a 12-in. circle; cut each circle into 12 wedges. Roll up wedges from the wide end and place point side down 2 in. apart on greased baking sheets. Curve ends to form crescents. Cover and let rise in a warm place until doubled, about 30 minutes.
4. Preheat oven to 350°. Bake until golden brown, 10-12 minutes Remove the rolls to wire racks.

1 ROLL 128 cal., 4g fat (3g sat. fat), 19mg chol., 107mg sod., 19g carb. (4g sugars, 1g fiber), 3g pro.

PIMIENTO GREEN BEANS

PREP 5 min. COOK 10 min.
MAKES 10 servings

- 2 lbs. fresh green beans, cut into 2-inch pieces
- 1 can (14½ oz.) chicken broth
- ½ cup chopped onion
- 1 jar (2 oz.) chopped pimientos, drained
- ½ tsp. salt
- ⅛ to ¼ tsp. pepper
- ¼ cup shredded Parmesan cheese

In a large saucepan, bring beans, broth and onion to a boil. Reduce heat; cover and cook until crisp-tender, 10-15 minutes. Drain. Stir in pimientos, salt and pepper. Sprinkle with Parmesan cheese.

¾ CUP 44 cal., 1g fat (0 sat. fat), 2mg chol., 336mg sod., 8g carb. (3g sugars, 3g fiber), 3g pro.

WINNING CRANBERRY GLAZED HAM

PREP 15 min. + marinating
BAKE 2½ hours MAKES 16 servings

- 2 cans (16 oz. each) whole-berry cranberry sauce
- 1 cup orange juice
- ⅓ cup steak sauce
- 2 Tbsp. canola oil
- 2 Tbsp. prepared mustard
- 2 Tbsp. brown sugar
- 1 fully cooked bone-in ham (7 to 9 lbs.)

1. In a large bowl, combine the cranberry sauce, orange juice, steak sauce, oil, mustard and brown sugar. Score the surface of the ham with shallow diagonal cuts, making diamond shapes.
2. Place the ham in a resealable 2-gal. bag. Add half of cranberry mixture; seal the bag and turn ham to coat. Refrigerate ham 8 hours or overnight, turning it a few times. Refrigerate the remaining cranberry mixture.
3. Preheat oven to 325°. Drain ham, discarding marinade. Place ham on rack in roasting pan lined with foil; cover the pan with additional foil. Bake for 1¾ hours.
4. Place the reserved cranberry mixture in a small saucepan; heat through. Uncover ham; brush with cranberry mixture.
5. Bake until a thermometer reads 140°. Heat 45-60 minutes longer, brushing with cranberry mixture every 15 minutes. Warm remaining cranberry mixture; serve with ham.

4 OZ. 264 cal., 7g fat (2g sat. fat), 87mg chol., 1164mg sod., 22g carb. (15g sugars, 1g fiber), 29g pro.

GRANDMA'S SPRITZ COOKIES

PREP 15 min. **BAKE** 10 min./batch
MAKES 6½ dozen

- 1 **cup shortening**
- ¾ **cup sugar**
- 1 **large egg, room temperature**
- 1 **tsp. almond extract**
- 2¼ **cups all-purpose flour**
- ½ **tsp. baking powder**
  Dash salt
  Optional: Assorted sprinkles and colored sugar

1. Preheat oven to 400°. In a large bowl, cream shortening and sugar until light and fluffy, 5-7 minutes. Add egg and almond extract; mix well. Combine the flour, baking powder and salt; add to creamed mixture until blended.

2. Using a cookie press fitted with your preferred disk, press dough shapes 2 in. apart onto ungreased baking sheets. If desired, sprinkle with toppings. Bake until set (do not brown), 7-8 minutes.

1 COOKIE 44 cal., 3g fat (1g sat. fat), 2mg chol., 6mg sod., 5g carb. (2g sugars, 0 fiber), 0 pro.

CHOCOLATE-PEANUT BUTTER TOPPERS

PREP 30 min.
BAKE 15 min./batch + cooling
MAKES 5 dozen

- 1 **cup butter, softened**
- ½ **cup sugar**
- 2 **tsp. vanilla extract**
- 2 **cups all-purpose flour**
  Additional sugar

PEANUT BUTTER TOPPING
- ⅓ **cup packed brown sugar**
- ⅓ **cup creamy peanut butter**
- ¼ **cup butter, softened**

CHOCOLATE GLAZE
- ½ **cup semisweet chocolate chips, melted**
- ⅓ **cup confectioners' sugar**
- 2 **Tbsp. 2% milk**

1. Preheat oven to 325°. In a large bowl, cream butter and sugar until light and fluffy, 5-7 minutes. Beat in vanilla. Gradually add flour to creamed mixture and mix well.

2. Shape dough into ¾-in. balls. Coat bottom of a glass with cooking spray, then dip in sugar. Flatten cookies with prepared glass, dipping glass in sugar as needed. Place on baking sheets. Bake until set, 12-15 minutes. Remove cookies to wire racks to cool completely.

3. In a small bowl, beat the brown sugar, peanut butter and butter until smooth. Spread 1 tsp. over each cookie. Combine glaze ingredients; gently spread ¾ tsp. over each peanut butter layer. Store in a single layer in airtight containers.

1 COOKIE 157 cal., 10g fat (6g sat. fat), 20mg chol., 75mg sod., 16g carb. (9g sugars, 1g fiber), 2g pro.

CRANBERRY SWEET ROLLS

PREP 55 min. + rising **BAKE** 25 min.
MAKES 15 rolls

- 1¼ cups sugar, divided
- ½ cup water
- 2 cups cranberries
- 1 tsp. grated orange zest
- 2 pkg. (¼ oz. each) active dry yeast
- ½ cup warm water (110° to 115°)
- ½ cup butter, softened
- ½ cup whole milk
- 2 large eggs, room temperature
- 1 tsp. salt
- 1 tsp. ground cinnamon
- ½ tsp. ground nutmeg
- 4½ to 5 cups all-purpose flour
  Melted butter

CREAM CHEESE FROSTING

- 1 cup confectioners' sugar
- 3 Tbsp. cream cheese, softened
- ½ tsp. vanilla extract
- ½ tsp. whole milk
- ¼ cup butter, softened

1. In a large saucepan, bring ¾ cup sugar and the water to a boil. Add the cranberries; return to a boil. Cook, uncovered, until cranberries begin to pop, about 6 minutes. Reduce heat; simmer until thickened, about 15 minutes, stirring occasionally. Stir in orange zest. Cover and chill.
2. In a large bowl, dissolve yeast in warm water. Add the next 6 ingredients, plus the remaining ½ cup sugar and 3 cups flour; beat until smooth. Add enough remaining flour to form a soft dough. Turn dough onto a floured surface; knead until smooth and elastic, 6-8 minutes. Place in a greased bowl; turning once to grease top. Cover and let rise in a warm place until doubled, about 1 hour. Preheat oven to 375°.
3. Punch dough down. Roll it out into a 15x10-in. rectangle; brush with butter. Spread cranberry

filling over dough to within 1 in. of edge. Roll up, jelly roll style, starting at long side.
4. Cut into 15 slices; place cut side down in a greased 13x9-in. baking pan. Cover dough and let rise until doubled, about 30 minutes.
5. Bake until golden brown, 25-30 minutes. Cool in pan for

5 minutes; remove to a wire rack to cool completely.
6. In a small bowl, beat frosting ingredients until smooth; spread frosting over warm rolls.

1 ROLL 356 cal., 12g fat (7g sat. fat), 60mg chol., 281mg sod., 56g carb. (26g sugars, 2g fiber), 6g pro.

GRANDMA'S SEAFOOD CHOWDER

PREP 15 min. **COOK** 25 min.
MAKES 10 servings (about 3 quarts)

3	Tbsp. plus ¼ cup butter, divided
1	lb. sliced fresh mushrooms
⅓	cup all-purpose flour
1	tsp. salt
⅛	tsp. pepper
4	cups half-and-half cream
1½	cups 2% milk
1	lb. haddock fillets, skin removed, cut into 1-inch pieces
1	lb. uncooked medium shrimp, peeled and deveined
2	cups frozen peas (about 10 oz.)
¾	cup shredded cheddar cheese
1	cup lump crabmeat (about 5 oz.), drained
1	jar (4 oz.) diced pimientos, drained
1	tsp. paprika

1. In a 6-qt. stockpot, heat 3 Tbsp. butter over medium-high heat. Add mushrooms. Cook and stir until tender, 8-10 minutes. Remove from pot.

2. In same pot, heat remaining ¼ cup butter over medium heat. Stir in flour, salt and pepper until smooth; gradually whisk in cream and milk. Bring to a boil, stirring constantly; cook and stir until thickened, 2-3 minutes.

3. Stir in haddock, shrimp, peas and sauteed mushrooms; cook until fish just begins to flake easily with a fork and shrimp turn pink, 5-7 minutes.

4. Add cheddar cheese, crab and diced pimientos; stir gently until cheddar is melted. Sprinkle each serving with paprika.

1¼ CUPS 390 cal., 23g fat (14g sat. fat), 176mg chol., 596mg sod., 14g carb. (8g sugars, 2g fiber), 28g pro.

CRISP CANDY CANE COOKIES

PREP 25 min. + chilling
BAKE 10 min./batch **MAKES** 3 dozen

- ½ cup butter, softened
- ⅓ cup sugar
- ⅓ cup packed brown sugar
- 1 large egg, room temperature
- 1 tsp. vanilla extract
- 1¼ cups all-purpose flour
- 1 tsp. baking powder
- ¼ tsp. salt
- 5 candy canes, crushed
- ½ cup white chocolate chips, melted

1. In a large bowl, cream butter and sugars until light and fluffy, 5-7 minutes. Beat in egg and vanilla. Combine flour, baking powder and salt; gradually add to creamed mixture and mix well. Stir in crushed candy canes. Cover and refrigerate 30 minutes.

2. Preheat oven to 375°. Divide dough into 36 pieces; shape each into a 4-in. rope. Place dough ropes 2 in. apart on greased baking sheets; curve the top of each to form a candy cane.

3. Bake until edges are lightly browned, 8-10 minutes. Cool cookies for about 2 minutes before removing to wire racks to cool completely. Drizzle with melted white chocolate. If desired, sprinkle with additional crushed candy canes. Let set before serving.

1 COOKIE 66 cal., 3g fat (2g sat. fat), 12mg chol., 54mg sod., 10g carb. (6g sugars, 0 fiber), 1g pro.

CHEDDAR-PECAN CRISPS

PREP 25 min. + chilling
BAKE 15 min./batch + cooling
MAKES 24 dozen

- 2 cups unsalted butter, softened
- 4 cups shredded sharp cheddar cheese
- 4½ cups all-purpose flour
- 1 tsp. salt
- ½ tsp. garlic powder
- ½ tsp. cayenne pepper
- 1 cup finely chopped pecans, toasted

1. Cream butter and cheese until light and fluffy, 3-4 minutes. Whisk together flour, salt, garlic powder and cayenne. Gradually beat those ingredients into the creamed mixture. Stir in pecans.

2. Cut dough into 8 pieces; roll each piece into a 10-in.-long log. Wrap securely. Refrigerate until dough is firm, about 2 hours.

3. Preheat oven to 350°. Unwrap and cut dough into ¼-in. slices. Place 1 in. apart on ungreased baking sheets. Bake until edges are crisp and lightly browned, 12-14 minutes. Cool on pans about 1 minute. Remove to wire racks to cool completely. Refrigerate crisps in airtight containers.

FREEZE OPTION Put wrapped logs in freezer containers; place in the freezer. To use, unwrap frozen logs and slice. If necessary, let stand 15 minutes at room temperature before cutting. Bake as directed, increasing time by 1-2 minutes.

1 CRISP 27 cal., 2g fat (1g sat. fat), 5mg chol., 19mg sod., 2g carb. (0 sugars, 0 fiber), 1g pro.

Handcrafted

CREATE A FEELING OF HOME

ANGELIC FAVOR BOXES

WHAT YOU'LL NEED

Templates (p. 2)

Patterned card stock

Painter's tape

String

Ribbon, pipe cleaners, pompoms or other frills, optional

Craft knife with cutting mat

Ruler

Hole punch

Hot glue gun

DIRECTIONS

1. Print and cut out template following the outside lines.

2. Place the template on back of card stock and secure with tape. Cut around the outer edge of the template. Remove the tape and template.

3. Mark the score lines with a soft pencil, using a ruler as a guide. Use the craft knife to gently score the marked lines.

4. Punch 2 small holes on opposite sides of the design (shown on template).

5. Fold over the tabbed edges and fold up the sides to create a pyramid shape. Apply hot glue to folded tabs, 1 side at a time. Leave 1 of the sides of the box open (choose a side with a hole punched in it).

6. Fill the box with candy, toys or treats. Close it gently, making sure the tabs are folded in.

7. Thread string through holes, going through the assembled side of the box first and out through the open wall. Tie or twist to secure.

8. Glue decorations or wings (see template) to box if desired.

BUTTON ORNAMENTS

WHAT YOU'LL NEED

Buttons

Embroidery floss

Festive embellishments,
such as ribbons or stars

Needle

Scissors

DIRECTIONS

1. Stack spare buttons in the desired order.

2. Holding them in place, use a needle to string coordinating colored embroidery floss through from top to bottom. Be sure to leave a long tail of floss at the top of the stack.

3. Bring the needle and floss back up through the buttons to the top, this time using a button hole positioned opposite the first.

4. Trim the working end of the floss, leaving a few inches to knot the tails together and form a loop for hanging.

5. Add festive embellishments, as desired.

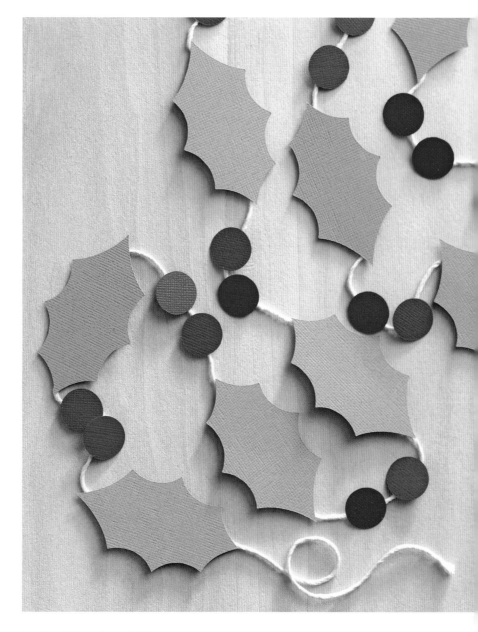

RED AND GREEN GARLAND

WHAT YOU'LL NEED

Card stock (green and red)

White twine or string

Cricut machine

Fast-dry craft glue or hot glue gun

DIRECTIONS

1. Select a holly shape and a berry shape in Cricut Design Space. (These can be found by searching in "Images.") Cut out shapes as needed from the card stock. (For a 6-foot-long garland, you'll need about 14 leaves and 26 berries.) Alternatively, make this craft with a standard printer: Search for berry and holly leaf templates online and cut out the shapes with scissors.

2. Glue string to one side of each leaf and berry, using an alternating pattern. Dry thoroughly.

"With the new day comes new strength and new thoughts."

— ELEANOR ROOSEVELT

Though its blades may be rusty and creaky, it still pulls as much water as you can pump on a given day. I took this photo in early summer, just as the sun was peeking over the horizon.

KELLIE CARTER NEWCASTLE, OK